IVP
CLASSICS

How to Give Away Your Faith

EXPANDED AND UPDATED BY MARIE LITTLE

PAUL E. LITTLE

FOREWORD BY LEE STROBEL

IVP Books

An imprint of InterVarsity Press
Downers Grove, Illinois

S0-BNU-361

InterVarsity Press
P.O. Box 1400, Downers Grove, IL 60515-1426
World Wide Web: www.ivpress.com
E-mail: email@ivpress.com

*InterVarsity Press® is the book-publishing division of InterVarsity Christian Fellowship/USA®, a
student movement active on campus at hundreds of universities, colleges and schools of nursing in the
United States of America, and a member movement of the International Fellowship of Evangelical
Students. For information about local and regional activities, write Public Relations Dept.,
InterVarsity Christian Fellowship/USA, 6400 Schroeder Rd., P.O. Box 7895, Madison, WI
53707-7895, or visit the IVCF website at <www.intervarsity.org>.*

Design: Cindy Kiple
Images: Henrick Sorenson/Getty Images

ISBN-10: 0-8308-3406-0
ISBN-13: 978-0-8308-3406-8

Printed in the United States of America ∞

Library of Congress Cataloging-in-Publication Data

Little, Paul E.
  How to give away your faith / Paul Little.
     p. cm.
  Includes bibliographical references.
  ISBN-13: 978-0-8308-3406-8 (pbk.: alk. paper)
  ISBN-10: 0-8308-3406-0 (pbk.: alk. paper)
  1. Witness bearing (Christianity) I. Title.
  BV4520.L5 2007
  248'.5—dc22

                                                                    2006030485

P	16	15	14	13	12	11	10	9	8	7	6	5	4	3	2	1
Y	19	18	17	16	15	14	13	12	11	10	09	08	07	06		

Contents

Foreword by Lee Strobel 7

Foreword by Leighton Ford. 11

Preface 15

1 THE ESSENTIAL FOUNDATION 19

2 THE EFFECTIVE AMBASSADOR 45

3 HOW TO WITNESS 61

4 HURDLING SOCIAL BARRIERS 88

5 WHAT IS OUR MESSAGE? 104

6 WHY WE BELIEVE 125

7 CHRIST IS RELEVANT TODAY 159

8 WORLDLINESS: EXTERNAL OR INTERNAL? 173

9 LIVING BY FAITH 192

10 FEEDING THE SPRING 207

Notes 227

Foreword

————— ❧ —————

I was working as an editor at a Chicago area newspaper. My boss knew that I was a Christian, but we had never discussed the issue. Then at the end of a horribly hectic day during which nearly everybody had lost his or her composure, he said to me: "Strobel, how did you get through the day without blowing your top? What's this Christianity thing to you?"

Nobody had ever asked me that before. I wasn't sure what to say, but I walked over to his office door, closed it and spent the next forty-five minutes telling him as best I could how Jesus Christ had brought me from atheism to faith and radically redirected the trajectory of my life.

It was one of the most exhilarating encounters I had ever experienced! When I emerged, I felt as if my entire life had been a movie shot in very grainy black-and-white film with scratchy sound—yet that forty-five minutes had been filmed in vivid Technicolor with rich Dolby stereo.

I instantly realized that sharing the gospel was one of the most exciting, fulfilling and important endeavors of the Christian life. But one thing was clear: to be effective in telling others about Jesus, I was going to need some help. Rather than merely bumbling around like I did with my boss, I wanted to be able to naturally and persuasively talk about Christianity as God opened up opportunities for me.

That's why I was so glad that a friend gave me a copy of Paul Little's book *How to Give Away Your Faith*. Here was a treasure trove of sage advice, practical suggestions and theological wisdom—all written by Paul Little, one of the most winsome and accomplished evangelists of our time. He wasn't merely an armchair expert; rather, Little consistently and creatively lived out Jesus' command that his followers spread the good news far and wide.

Little was killed in a car accident in 1975. Ironically, though, I later became friends with his widow, Marie, who attended the same church where I had found Christ. Like Paul, Marie enthusiastically shared Christ with others and mentored Christians in how they could do the same. In fact, she later used Paul's lecture notes—and her own formidable knowledge and experience—in updating this classic volume.

Now, many years after that life-changing meeting with my boss, I'm still thankful for the role that this immensely helpful book played in giving me the confidence to engage in spiritual conversations. One thing hasn't changed—I still find that sharing the gospel is one of the most satisfying and rewarding aspects of the Christian faith.

Whether you're already an outreach veteran or frightened at the prospect of talking to someone about Jesus, you'll find this book to be an invaluable resource. Like me, you'll marvel at how Paul and Marie have been able to synthesize so much useful and encouraging material into one easy-to-read volume.

So read on—and get ready to go from black-and-white living to the colorful adventure of personal evangelism!

Lee Strobel
Author of The Case for Christ
Fall 2006

Foreword

In the last twenty-five years the publishing of Christian books has grown at an enormous pace. It is now estimated there are more than two thousand new titles out every year!

The question comes: How many of these are going to be read at all and how few will be circulated for more than a year or so? So when a book is republished after a quarter of a century, that speaks powerfully about its significance.

I well remember a youth conference we held in Moncton, New Brunswick, Canada, during the Christmas holidays of 1963. Several hundred Canadian young people had gathered "for a Real Cool Yule" as we called it! Paul Little was one of the speakers at the conference. In my office hangs a classic photo of Paul, me and other members of the team looking pretty worn out after a pick-up basketball game at that conference.

One late evening after the activities were over, a number of us sat around a table for a snack. Paul was telling us about a book on evangelism that he had written and was looking for something that would grab as a title. It happened that I had just been reading a message by Robert Spear, the great missions leader in the early part of this century. Robert Spear used to say to audiences, "You say you have a faith in Christ? Then either give it away or give it out." We began to play around with that thought. As I recall, I suggested the title, *How to Give Your Faith Away,* and eventually the book appeared under the current title *How to Give Away Your Faith.*

I tell that story not just for the sake of reminiscence, but to say that I am deeply grateful to have had a small share in what is an enduring classic in personal evangelism.

Paul Little was one of my closest friends. We worked together in student university missions. He was the program director and I the program chairman at the Lausanne Congress on World Evangelization in 1974. When he was killed in a car accident the next summer, it was one of the most moving and difficult but special experiences of my life to be asked to speak at his funeral and memorial service.

Not only did and do I love Paul and his wife, Marie, but I learned so much from him. I still turn to *How to Give Away Your Faith* to refresh my mind on some of those sharp ideas and insights and stories and approaches that Paul was so filled with.

Over the years I have recommended this book to countless hundreds of people, and I know many have been helped by it. So I count it a real privilege to write an introduction for this revised edition. I am grateful that Paul's wife, Marie, has brought it up to date and incorporated some of Paul's material that has not been used before and added some contemporary illustrations, including one about our own son Sandy.

I also commend InterVarsity Press for bringing out this fresh edition. It is my prayer that God will use this book to motivate, instruct and lead believers in this generation to share a living faith with friends and neighbors, here and around the world, who still have a deep heart hunger for God, but often don't know what it is they are longing for.

One of Paul's favorite messages was about David who "served God in his own generation and fell asleep." Paul has fallen asleep. He served God in his own generation. I pray that God may use this book to help readers in this generation to be lively, authentic and credible witnesses for Christ.

Leighton Ford
Charlotte, North Carolina
1988

Preface

---- ❦ ----

I have spent the last eight months tampering with genius. At least at times that's how I felt as I worked to update a book which has sold a million copies and continues to sell at a steady pace.

I think I can rightly use the word *genius* in talking about my husband, Paul. Unlike many armchair evangelists, Paul did what a lot of us wish we could do. He was able to make the Christian message comprehensible and alive to students and others as he traveled to hundreds of campuses throughout the world. He was warmly dubbed by one friend as "a shirt-sleeve evangelist." He didn't just talk about witnessing; he did it! And it was from the lessons he learned in his persistent witness that this book originally came about. He described it as "a book on instruction rather than exhortation" to witness.

Now, two decades later, the fundamentals Paul taught with his eye-opening illustrations hold firmly true and are still eminently useful. And timeless—perhaps even before their time.

Twenty years ago Paul told us what to say to a man who tells you that a fried egg on his ear gives him joy, peace and happiness. His answer could be the same today for someone who tells you that a crystal on his or her chest brings light to life.

Paul's unfaltering relevance, along with the book's practicality, convinced the editors at InterVarsity Press and me that *How to Give Away Your Faith* was worth updating . . . and worth maintaining at its highest potential. The cultural shifts from the sixties to the near nineties made certain quotations and applications out of date for our time. Moreover, I knew there was later material from Paul's tapes and notes that he had envisioned using one day to write *How to Give Away Your Faith II*.

Fortunately, Paul left a wealth of material that would make such a revision possible. Spurred on by the editors, I began to comb through his tapes and files and soon discovered "vintage Paul Little" material not yet in print. His original tapes of "The Effective Ambassador" (which became the Twentyonehundred slide presentation bearing that name) now enhance chapter two. Other new items include

- three questions for finding out where people are on their spiritual journeys

- instructions for following up with a new Christian

- how to dispel some popular misconceptions of Christianity

- and many illustrations of practical truths.

In every case I have sought to maintain Paul's major thrust for the book and have guarded every expression that carries his special flavor. Yet it will be obvious in some of the present-day references that the insertions are from my own research and experience.

Were Paul alive today he would probably shake his head at the original book and my efforts to preserve it, saying in self-deprecation, "I don't know that these are deathless words." In this case, I would surely disagree with him, for the more I mulled over his material, the more my own motivation heightened to continue witnessing to the life-changing power of Jesus Christ. My solemn prayer is that each reader may respond similarly.

One discovery helped to dispel the fears and inadequacies I felt about this undertaking. I learned that every one of Oswald Chambers's prolific writings were published posthumously. During his lectures between 1907 and 1917, his wife took shorthand notes from which all of his books were produced after his death in his early forties. Paul was in his late forties when an automobile accident took him to heaven while our family was on vacation. There were some obvious parallels in our two stories. I took this widow's model as the Lord's prompting to undertake this update. And now my prayer with this edition is that all who read will come to the same deep conviction as Paul that "the greatest favor you can do for others is to introduce them to Jesus Christ."

Marie Little
Prospect Heights, Illinois

1

The Essential Foundation

So you want to witness! I did too, but I didn't have a clue how to do it without stubbing my toe in the process.

How about you? Do you know how to make the good news relevant? Do you know how to communicate to people to whom the gospel seems alien? How do you talk about Jesus Christ to . . .

- the religion major who mocks your defense of biblical teachings with, "But this is the twentieth century, John!"?
- the hard-working manager of the local service station?
- that office worker who's just been replaced by a thinking machine?
- the junior who's ready to drop out of school because of drug abuse?
- the "who cares" party boy across the hall?
- that girl you know who's gotten everything she's ever wanted?

- those nearest to you: your family, your friends, your next-door neighbors?
- the man on the street who would be one of the 150 million casualties during the first eighteen hours of a nuclear war?
- the trapped housewife struggling to keep up with small children, the Joneses and a dozen civic demands?
- the victim of divorce or abuse who can't trust anyone?
- the doctor who has fertilized a human egg in a test tube and successfully transplanted it in a surrogate mother?
- the upwardly mobile professional next to you in the office?

It's easy to quote "God so loved the world . . . ," but what do the words mean? What can you say that will make sense to these people in their everyday lives?

REALISM IS ESSENTIAL

To begin with, we must be realistic about the world we live in. Times are changing faster than ever before in history. Although Jesus Christ remains the same yesterday, today and forever, these changes significantly color the attitudes and receptivity of those to whom we witness.

My generation grew up playing cowboys and Indians, cops and robbers, paper dolls and store. Today's children live their lives with a ceaseless background of TV while playing out elaborate fantasies with "supernaturals," ghosts and transformers. As they get older, children are becoming all but submerged in an ocean of video games and electronic music.

Today's adults have their own sets of electronic toys; each year new ones arrive, outdating last year's. In addition, the information explosion has turned the entire world into a single "global village" and given everyone a front seat at major events around the world. As a result people are exposed to a cafeteria of cultures and mores; all they have to do is choose what to believe. Along with this, the ever-present media spew out images of a future of genetic mapping, brain-code exploration and "green machines" to produce food from sunlight and air alone. Far and away the most universal change in recent years has been the computerization and miniaturization of every area of life.

But while we have made quantum leaps in our hopes to mold and conquer the universe, the future of civilization seems less and less certain. Is it inevitable that nuclear war will wipe out the whole human race? Will environmental damage threaten the future habitability of the earth? Or will the spread of AIDS bring slow, painful death even if we conquer other threats? And what is the future of the disintegrating American family?

All this reminds us of the little boy's statement, "If I live to be a man, I'll . . ." Inherent in his statement is the crucial question, Will we all survive and will America make it? Until recently, the trend has been to turn to the gee-whiz wonders of science and technology. High tech is everywhere we look—in the factory, office and home. Its plastic, miracle-working boxes have seduced us into thinking that technology can solve everything. But the truth is, it fails in the most crucial aspect, our need for personal concern and touch. We cannot live by technology alone! Nor can our obsessive consumerism bring hoped-for solace. As a film star once observed, "How many toasters can one person use?"

Now an alarming number of people are looking for honest answers in the new self-help or human potential movements. On close inspection, these are far from innocent twenty-four-hour cures. They promise personal effectiveness and motivational training through Eastern-influenced "mind control" techniques that on the surface appear harmless. Underneath, their values are alien to Christianity. In their groups they spin tales about past lives by using trance channelers, mantras and divining crystals while their Hindu and occultist roots go undetected. Along with this they foster moral anarchy, each person seeking his own truth, blithely bypassing God's revealed truth. Philosophically, their base is monism; we are all gods, humanity is god and all religions are one. The fact that the movement has attracted so many followers reveals a yawning vacuum in the lives of people who are reaching and searching for a possible source of salvation.

Salvation? From what? Loneliness and isolation is the answer we hear from young people. In the sixties, young people began their search with demonstrations and revolutions. They hoped to find meaning in doing their own thing. In the seventies, a spent generation turned into the narcissistic "me" generation. And that spawned the generation of the eighties which seems to be content, by and large, with a materialistic, value-free society.

Listen to a description of the university world of this decade:

> Almost every student entering university believes or says he believes that truth is relative. They fear not error, but intolerance. They ask, "What right do I or anyone else have to say one (culture or religion) is better than another?" . . . Spiritual entropy or an evaporation of the soul's boiling blood is taking place. . . . Respect for the sacred, real religion and knowledge of the Bible have diminished to the vanishing point.[1]

This comes, not from an evangelical preacher, but from University of Chicago professor Allan Bloom.

This spiritual entropy, as Bloom puts it, has penetrated every level of our society. For instance, American high-school students have all but stated that for them, celebrity counts for everything. A 1987 World Almanac poll listed their ten heroes. In order of preference the winners were: Bill Cosby, Sylvester Stallone, Eddie Murphy, Ronald Reagan, Chuck Norris, Clint Eastwood, Molly Ringwald, Rob Lowe, Arnold Schwarzenegger and Don Johnson.[2] With the exception of President Ronald Reagan, they are all entertainers or actors. For the high schoolers, the conclusion is unmistakable: if you are not famous (or not in show business), you are nothing. And the implication is that they also admire and would like to imitate their lifestyles.

Adults are not immune from this spiritual entropy either. *Time* magazine's cover story of May 25, 1987, tells of more than a hundred government officials who have ethical or legal charges against them. *Time* also named Wall Street pinstriped millionaires who are under indictment for illegally manipulating millions of dollars to their own benefit. Besides that, *Time* describes an appalling list of marines, televangelists and presidential candidates indicted or dethroned because of illicit relationships. The writers of *Time* (not the preachers) headline their story with "Whatever happened to ethics?"

Students, Ph.D.s, blue-collar and white-collar workers, parents, doctors, statesmen, your neighbors and mine are all mired in the same bog of shifting values.

Today's adults

- are hard-working.
- are struggling for financial security.
- can be generous and helpful to neighbors.

- make pleasure and leisure priorities.
- are committed to causes that generally line up with their self-interests.
- hate to be patronized.
- can easily detect a hidden agenda in relationships.
- will resist high pressure from any group.
- if single, may flock to bars for human contact and solace.

Religiously, these adults

- see science as more reliable than religion.
- consider Christianity's claim to uniqueness to be bigoted in the extreme.
- find their moral certainty has either shifted downward or vanished entirely.
- believe psychology probably has as many answers as religion.
- view God as a stern judge or a benign, distant grandfather.
- believe God is probably irrelevant to their existence.
- rarely see the Bible as a source of help.
- vaguely wonder if there isn't some truth to the new cults.
- see Christians as judgmental killjoys.
- will quickly point to the hypocrisy of so-called people of God on TV who bilk money from supporters.

These same adults

- if graduating from college, fear that they won't find a job.
- worry about the risks of marital commitments.
- doubt that their family relationships will ever be stable and satisfying.

- are tempted to abandon traditional values.
- face relentless competition for success.
- fear that they will be part of the grim statistics of people pushed out of their jobs after age forty.
- wonder if they will lose their looks and be rejected.
- worry that old age will find them alone and disabled.

This picture, although not comprehensive, is not pretty. It describes, nonetheless, the kind of soil in which we sow the truth of Jesus Christ. These trends and pressures affect Christians as well as those who have not yet trusted Jesus Christ. Furthermore, I have not intended to imply by this picture that Christians are a holy breed free from any flaws. Far from it! We, too, can be caught up by the same pressures and cultural drifts.

CHRISTIANITY IS REALISTIC

We Christians cannot live with our heads in a bucket and ignore the truth of this picture. It should be no surprise to us when we hear stories of abuse and violence happening in our own neighborhoods. More important, we must be convinced beyond all doubt that the Christian faith has a message for all facets of this world, that its truth has transformed our lives and that it is of supreme value for everyone.

Any temptation to avoid understanding our world is comparable to the philosophies claiming all reality (including sin) is in the mind. The Christian faith is not so spiritual and other-worldly that it denies this world's reality or the existence of matter. The Christian faith affirms material things; yet it sees beyond them to spiritual things, the ultimate reality.

Jesus Christ dealt with the crux of this reality question when he fed the five thousand with five loaves and two fish. Jesus saw the crowd's need and fed them. The people were stunned by this miraculous feat and wanted to draft him as their leader. What a windfall to have a king like this! But our Lord withdrew from them, as he always did when people were following him for the wrong reasons. When they found him the next day, he told them they were following him only because they had eaten their fill. Then he spoke to the issue of the material versus the spiritual: "Do not work for food that spoils, but for food that endures to eternal life, which the Son of Man will give you" (John 6:27).

Jesus was teaching that material food is real. Hunger is real. The world of cities and streets, rocks and trees and people does exist. But he was emphasizing that spiritual realities are of pre-eminent value; they transcend and outlast the material. Indeed, they give true meaning to the material world.

Of course Jesus knew that the people were famished. So he used real food to feed them. He didn't just pray for them and then send them home hungry. He saw them as whole people, not as mere "souls," somehow separated from the rest of themselves. He also knew that their physical and emotional needs were tightly bound up with their spiritual hungers. After they had listened to his message, Jesus then demonstrated that he cared about their material needs as well. In many cases, he dealt with the physical needs first!

This causes us to think deeply about the extraordinary sensitivity Jesus had for the needs of all people, whether he met them in large groups or in individual encounters. It brings us to ask what steps we must take to follow his example. First, we must be aware of the condition of those around us—whether they are hungry, tired, bored, lonely, mistreated or rejected. We must try to understand what and how they think, how they feel, what they aspire to be and do.

I will never forget an Asian man, a judge, who chatted with me in the dining commons of Harvard University. Speaking as a Christian, he said, "I wish you Christians in the West could realize that we from the East, who have gone through the ravages of war, starvation, suffering, political turmoil and the loss of loved ones, have a profound wound in our hearts." And he continued, "I know that essentially the gospel is God's message of love and that while it has social implications, it is directed primarily to man's spiritual need for redemption. But it would mean so much if only we saw that you understood this wound in our hearts."

Many of those we rub shoulders with carry just such a "profound wound" in their hearts. Their response to us and the good news we share depends a lot on whether they think we really understand and care. An old Indian proverb states it, "One man should say nothing to another until he has walked in his moccasins." In spirit, at least, we need to sit and walk where they walk. When we can repeat back to them their thoughts and feelings in our own words, they will begin to trust us. From there they will be willing to think seriously about the things we care about.

It should not surprise us that the people whom God has greatly used throughout the centuries have not just known their Bibles well; they have known other people well, too. And loving both, they have made the Word relevant to others.

Because we as Christians have the privilege of knowing the answer to our world's needs, this can be an exciting time to witness. We probably agree, we *should* witness, even that we *must* witness. But when the time comes, we ask the big question, *How* can we witness? How can we explain clearly to this world that Jesus Christ is a right and relevant solution today? On what grounds can we approach those who touch our lives and expect to be heard—and believed?

Start with the Person Next Door

To develop Jesus' kind of sensitivity can only be done by having man-to-man or woman-to-woman contact. As Christians we must turn from the world at large to the person next door. Herein lies the rub, for as the old saying goes:

> To love the world to me's no chore,
> My trouble is the man next door.

Unequivocally, it is when we get involved personally with others that our evangelism begins to take off. Unless we stop theorizing and reach out and knock on the neighbor's door, we'll never get to the real nuts and bolts of witnessing. Lifestyle evangelism begins with talking to people who in some way touch our lives. It is not a superficial, quick relationship or an overnight coup. It involves time and sacrifice, and most of all it involves giving ourselves.

Listen

An easy first step for any of us to take is to start to listen to those around us. I said *listen* not *talk!* Stop long enough just to hear. It might take some effort because it's easier to give advice and talk about our own experiences than to think about the other person. If you are naturally shy, focus your thoughts on the feelings and concerns of the people you're trying to reach. Are they feeling uncomfortable? Do they find it difficult to converse? What are their concerns? Refuse to allow yourself to dwell on your own emotions. You will find yourself projecting warmth and concern for the other person. As someone has said, "Listen with your heart, not your mind."

In my work of lecturing to college and university students, I like to sit in student lounges and interact casually with all kinds of students. When I hear the specifics of what they are thinking and how they spend their out-of-class time, I see the real world. Or as I travel, I have the opportunity to hear my fellow travelers tell of their lives away from home. Their comments are peppered with a surprising number of their fears. It's often an eye-opener. One man said he had both a wife and a mistress and couldn't understand why he wasn't happy. This is the real world and it pays to listen and learn. In the process we earn the right to tell our own story.

During a conversation I had with a friend, I learned a good lesson about the effort involved in listening. We had a mutual acquaintance who was obviously searching for God. Feeling warm and concerned about that person, I suggested that perhaps I might call him sometime. My friend looked at me for a long moment and then advised, "Only call him if you're willing to be his friend." I got his message. If my attitude was "Well, I'll call and give him a gospel shot in the arm," I should forget it. Too many Christians evangelize as if they had a "gospel pill" to offer. If non-Christians would take it, they'd find the Savior. Anyone would recoil from such "quick-fix" witnessing.

BE INFORMED

Along with listening, another step for realistic followers of Jesus' example is to keep informed about the world around us. This will help those of us who must honestly admit that we would have nothing to say if we were locked up for an hour with a non-Christian. Reading a weekly news magazine, listening to the evening news and learning our community's needs will give us common ground to build on.

As we expand our information base, we will see a slice of life different from our own. It will help us relate the gospel to real situations and to scratch where people itch. The information could help us understand a colleague at work when he confides about a child with a chemical dependency. Or it could give us insight into the dilemma of the single parent down the street who needs an adult friend for her young child. When our neighbor confides in us about his pregnant teen, we might be able to offer information and insight along with our promise of prayer support. Informed Christians will naturally begin caring about their community and world. And the wonderful result will be finding ourselves working shoulder to shoulder with the world that Jesus Christ came to redeem.

WHAT DO CHRISTIANS HAVE TO OFFER?

So far we've been looking at our world today and considering individual needs of human beings in it. We've seen how imperative it is that we know and understand something about both. But if we're going to be realistic Christians, we have to take a careful look at our own spiritual dimension too.

What do we have to offer? Some time ago I spent the evening with a couple who had attended our church for a brief period, went to most of the activities, but then suddenly dropped out entirely. Some of us were concerned to know why these people left our church fellowship. During our conversation, as we discussed belonging to Jesus Christ and living for him, the husband became very thoughtful. He said, "You talk about a relationship with Jesus Christ that is supernatural. In your church, there are some people who have it and some people who don't." I was cut to the quick as I saw our group through the eyes of a visitor trying to search out this intangible "it." The difference was obvious to *him*.

Whether this man's evaluation was accurate or not, seekers are often carefully examining our Christian groups and us as individual Christians to find that eternal dimension we talk about. A superficial profession won't convince them. They're looking for the real thing—genuine, living faith. They don't always see it, though, in us individually or collectively. And this is not because they're spiritually blind, either. Sometimes it just isn't there.

IS THERE A DIFFERENCE IN THE CHRISTIAN?

Does our claim that we know Jesus Christ make a difference in our everyday lives, day in and day out—in our use of time, money and strength, and in our system of values? What happens Monday through Saturday? If we are students, how about the way we study and why we study? Does the faith we claim make a difference in our relationships with members of the opposite sex? Do we refuse to overindulge ourselves and exploit others? Do we respect people's integrity and rule out activities that demean others? Beyond that, how do we respond when we are disappointed or bereaved? When the chips are down, do non-Christians see in us an attitude of honesty and sincerity that they would like to have? Or are they more apt to say to themselves (as many justifiably have), "I've got enough problems of my own; don't bother me with yours!"? Finally, does knowing Jesus Christ influence our life choices—choosing a major, a career, a graduate school, a spouse, a job?

THE BUSY CHRISTIAN

The "ivory tower" label often given to the university professor or student can unwittingly become the lifestyle of Mr. and Mrs. Average Christian. They can be isolated by the multitude of church activities, sometimes five nights a week. Kids' clubs, prayer meetings, music ministry, planning meetings, deacon and deaconess meetings—all very worthy activities. But the Average Christians may literally have no time for the unbelieving world. When they think about reaching their world, sheer busyness can prevent them from taking any action. We have all had the experience of wanting to witness but knowing down deep that no one was listening. The world will listen to our message when they see we have an ear that's tuned in.

NO PHONY CHRISTIANS

Phony solutions will never sell to our non-Christian contemporaries. They are fed up with phony people, and they aren't fooled by the pious person whose religion goes only skin-deep. No force-feeding of superficial formulas will reach them. Nor are they attracted by naive wishful thinkers who aren't ready to face up to life's harsh realities of wickedness, weakness, temptation or greed. They are looking for something genuine enough to have meaning in the real world. If Christians can demonstrate evidence in their own lives that Jesus Christ has rescued them— that for them Jesus is a living, daily reality—that will be realistic Christianity!

THREE KINDS OF FAITH

As we considered what we have to offer our world, you may have found yourself cold and tentative about your own faith, without any strong motivation to witness. Let me suggest one startling possibility—that is, your faith could be strictly environmental, an outgrowth of your surroundings.

In all of our Christian groups we can see that people have varying degrees of commitment. I would like to suggest that there are three categories that people fall into. First, there are those who could be described as having "indoctrination faith." These are people who without making a personal commitment to Christ, go through all the motions, sing all the right hymns, have all the right answers about the gospel. They have been well schooled from early childhood in Sunday-school classes and kids' clubs and never missed a church service. Indoctrination faith could describe the kids who won all the Bible quizzes and can quote John 3:16 in five languages. They have absorbed every answer they've ever heard, can teach classes and give sermons. They've got all the information, but that's all they've got. This is indoctrination faith.

Second, there are those with a "conformity faith." This faith is largely an outgrowth of strong Christian surroundings. On Sunday these people go to Bible classes and worship services and hear the Bible expounded. During the week they attend other church meetings and contribute with the best of them. They may do all the right things and none of the wrong things— but only because of the external pressure of family and church. Some mysterious sort of osmosis is supposed to make these people "spiritual" but, in fact, there is no genuine desire from within.

When people with conformity faith get into situations where they are on their own and free to decide what they're going to do, they shed their faith like a raincoat. If they go away to college, their whole lifestyle changes. They move out of the safety zone where every activity is carefully structured and get a rude shock. Suddenly they're faced with the shallow superficiality of their Christian experience. Most likely it has been an unconscious drift into reliance on their environment (faith on a horizontal level).

On secular campuses, I have all too often met students, stripped of their familiar Christian environment of home and church, who were faltering and unsure of themselves. Their second-hand faith has slowly disintegrated because they have never known a personal, vertical relationship with Jesus Christ. Back home, everybody says, "Oh, Johnny and Susie have lost their faith at the terrible state university." We need to raise the awkward question, "Did Johnny and Susie lose saving faith, or did they have only indoctrination or conformity faith to begin with?"

When non-Christians look at people with conformity faith they see a reflection of their environment (which they do not share) but nothing more. And it doesn't impress them. They're not looking for an environment; they're looking for living faith.

Having come from a Christian background myself, I have found it helpful to ask on a regular basis, "Is there anything in my life that can be explained only because of God himself? Or is everything that has happened to me due to my background, surroundings and present circumstances? What if, a week from now, my environment should be completely different?"

Fortunately, there is a third level of faith that has been called "commitment faith." This third level describes those who recognize that to be a Christian is more than giving mental assent to the facts about the Lord Jesus Christ. Demons do that much, as James 2:19 tells us. They believe in one God and tremble. Merely believing the facts is not in itself saving faith. On the other hand, people who have commitment faith are genuine followers of Jesus Christ and are committed to him on a double-or-nothing basis.

For instance, university students may find themselves in an environment openly hostile to Christianity. They may hear challenges to their faith they've never thought of before, let alone known the answers to. But because they are committed to Jesus Christ unequivocally, they will be motivated to dig out the answers rather than cast off their faith. Faced with temptations they'd never experienced before, like Daniel, Shadrach, Meshach and Abednego when they were taken to Babylon, rather than being influenced by the environment, they exert an influence on the environment. What makes these students different? The difference is they have saving faith born of the Spirit from above.

OOZING INTO CHRISTIANITY

It is important to avoid a drift into environmental faith at any stage in life. We need to beware of the often-unconscious belief that people can "ooze" into Christianity. This harmful tendency develops easily, especially in Christian homes. Watching my own children when they were young gave me a live illustration. I remember Paul Jr. at age four skipping through the house singing, "I'm happy, happy, happy all day long because Jesus is my friend." I hoped he was happy most of the time, and I also like to think he viewed Jesus as his friend. But doubtless, he often sang that song unaware of its meaning, as so many of us do regularly. We sing truths that are not our own. This pattern of rote repetition without thought or meaning starts in childhood and can become a regular habit carried into our adult life.

It has been observed, wisely I think, that hymns and choruses make liars of us all. We sing of glorious Christian experiences as though they were our very own, and yet they are not. Hymns of commitment are probably the ones most often sung without putting the words into action. When we mouth truths without thought or meaning, it leads us to accept an unreal experience as the norm. Without realizing it, we're actually living a lie. It is lamentable that our rich heritage of Christian music may lead us to substitute a fiction for the real thing.

BELIEVING FACTS IS NOT ENOUGH

Believing the facts about Jesus can cause us unwittingly to accept intellectual belief as an end in itself. Hence, we miss the experience of being dynamically related to the Person who embodies these facts. Again, I've met more than a few college students who told me honestly, "I believe everything about Christ," but they had to add, "It doesn't mean a thing to me. My faith is like Pepsi that's lost its fizz." Why should life-as-a-Christian be like cold mashed potatoes? Why should it be insipid and burdensome as well? It shouldn't, but for some it is.

Have we forgotten that becoming and being a Christian, at its very heart, involves receiving, living with and responding to a person? To give mental assent to a list of propositions about Jesus Christ is not the same as knowing him personally. It would be like knowing all the facts about the president of the United States but not ever meeting him personally. For many of us, our backgrounds may have included many facts about Jesus Christ, without helping us reach him as a living, present person.

Two Essential Ingredients for Faith

To know Jesus Christ personally involves two things. The first thing is a commitment, a time when we make a conscious decision, "Yes, I do want to belong to you, Lord Jesus Christ." That commitment is a continual, lifetime involvement of one's self with the living Lord. By definition, a relationship is continual, involving our entire person—quite different from assent to facts but having no contact with Jesus Christ personally. Perhaps we've never made that big commitment, never personally invited him into our lives to be our living Lord and Savior. If not, then that's the beginning.

The second thing is love and obedience to our living Lord and Savior. It is unthinkable to consider a relationship with the Lord Jesus that is less than 100 percent. He is the spectacular Lord from heaven; he is the Lord of all the earth. When we let this fact get fully into the marrow of our bones, willing obedience to him is an incredible privilege.

Some of our Lord's most solemn words are recorded in Matthew 7:21 when he warns his disciples, "Not everyone who says to me, 'Lord, Lord,' will enter the kingdom of heaven, but only he who does the will of my Father who is in heaven." Here Jesus talks about our relationship to him as *entering the kingdom*. In other places it is called *the new birth*. To enter this relationship is not a matter of using correct vocabulary or going through the empty motions. It involves a clear resolve to do his will. As basic as that resolve is, he does not accept us and love us because of our obedience to him. But obedience is the evidence of a true

commitment to him as our Lord. The apostle John adds a helpful thought. He says that if we keep Jesus' commandments, "we
know that we have come to know him" (1 John 2:3). And the
whole letter of James amplifies this point.

Does Faith Need Action?

Faith, in its very nature, demands action. Faith *is* action. Belief
can be tested by action. For instance, suppose a wild-eyed man
ran into your room and said the building would be blown up in
five minutes. If you were still there five minutes later, we would
know that you really didn't believe him. If you did believe him,
you'd get out as fast as you could. We could tell by your actions
what you honestly believed.

Similarly, I might tell you I believe that Jesus Christ is the one
and only Savior, that life's full meaning can only be known
through him and that apart from him all people are under the
eternal condemnation of God. But if I go my merry way, ignore
his words and his will and live a life of complete self-indulgence,
I am not honestly believing or entering the kingdom in the biblical sense.

The Bible gives us many exciting illustrations of men and
women whose faith in God was obvious from their day-by-day
actions and decisions. Rahab is listed in Hebrews as having faith
when she welcomed the Israelite spies into her house. She allied
herself with God's people. Joseph literally gave the empty sleeve
to Potiphar's wife to avoid immorality. Moses abandoned the
pleasures and privileges of a son of Pharaoh to identify himself
with the afflicted people of God. Elijah boldly challenged the
prophets of Baal to a sacrificial contest saying, "The God who
answers by fire, let him be God." Then with apparent brashness

he proceeded to dump barrels of water on his sacrifices. He knew his living, powerful God would reply, and he did. Beaten and imprisoned, Paul and Silas sang hymns of praise to their God at midnight. These were not simply pious expressions but confessions and acts of faith from the warp and woof of their everyday lives.

HOW DO YOU TREAT GOD?

Our actions will be based on the answer to a simple question: How do you treat God? Do we consider God to be a living person or just a thing on a shelf? Have we that heart-hunger and thirst that compels us day by day to get away—alone with him—to study his Word and take time to talk to him in prayer? Sometimes we sing the old hymn "Sweet Hour of Prayer" and yet avoid prayer time like the plague. Are we honest with ourselves? Was it yesterday or was it a week ago, a month ago or a year ago that we last met with the Lord alone?

Non-Christians need to detect the supernatural quality of our Christian experiences. Then they will listen to our words about Jesus Christ and ask what it means to know him personally. Students have sometimes come to me after I have spoken to a group and asked, "How does it work? How can I have the kind of life you've been talking about? Is there any hope for me?" It's the greatest privilege to sit down and explain how forgiveness, cleansing and God's power can be theirs by committing themselves to Jesus Christ.

BE HONEST WITH YOURSELF

Each one of us has been reading through this chapter with different attitudes, different reactions, different conclusions. Some of us are convinced that our faith in the Lord Jesus Christ is genuine, but we want it to deepen and grow as our awareness of him increases. Others of us are remembering that our faith used to be much more vibrant than it is now. Or perhaps we're beginning to realize with a chill that our faith never has been any more than a mental assent to the facts about Jesus Christ and a social conformity to our Christian peers. All these years we've been concerned about the pieces of information, but not about Jesus himself. Quite frankly, we may even be questioning whether such a thing as genuine faith or a personal relationship with Jesus Christ is possible.

Whatever our individual situations, let's at least be honest with ourselves and not put up a front to impress someone else. In the presence of God we can each ask ourselves whether we have genuine faith, faith that's actually meaningful every day. If we can answer yes with assurance, we ought to thank God again for his goodness and grace and ask him to deepen and extend our faith in each experience of life. Those of us who aren't sure that our answer is yes, or who know that we must say no, can take a simple step. Come to Jesus and speak to him directly. Tell him that you want to know him and to have faith in him. And tell him that you are prepared to put yourself completely into his supremely capable hands.

No Halfway for the Christian

As I have indicated before, there is no halfway faith in Jesus Christ. Total and irrevocable commitment to Jesus Christ every day is the prerequisite for a vital relationship with him. When we begin to hold out on him in some area or to rebel against his will (even in some "minor" detail), our spiritual vitality suffers.

A spiritual short circuit causes a snag in communications. We say we're willing to witness for the Lord to our friends or to our coworkers. But we start with conditions, "Please, Lord, don't ask me to befriend Joe; anyone but him, Lord." Or, as one young medical student said, "I'll witness anywhere, Lord, except to my professional colleagues."

How prone we are to think that we know better than God! Or that we must choose between doing God's will and our own happiness. As if God wanted us to be miserable! Our heavenly Father loves us; Jesus Christ died for us; the indwelling Holy Spirit is his promise to us. Certainly the Triune God is not about to short-change us in life. The well-known Indian pastor Sundar Singh said it well, "The capital of heaven is the heart in which Jesus Christ sits enthroned as King." The deepest joy that can be known in our life comes from total commitment to Jesus Christ and his will for us.

Then, we will find that telling others about him is an incomparable experience. Let us ask the Lord Jesus (for the hundredth time, or the first time) to live in us as Lord and Savior and to fill our lives. From there we can ask him to give us inner boldness and vigor to give away our faith to others.

The joy and rewards of witnessing are superb. A businessman in our small group Bible study called me on the phone the day after a meeting. His words made my day. He told me that he had taken home the small book I'd given him to read. "There were five points in that book," he told me. "When it came to number five, I did what it told me to do. I prayed to Jesus Christ and told him I wanted him to have my whole life." Then he said, "Hey, this is the greatest!" I totally agreed. It's the greatest thing to commit yourself to Jesus Christ. And it's the greatest thing to tell others about him.

But, remember: to witness effectively we must be realistic—genuine in our knowledge of people in today's world and genuine in our total commitment to Jesus Christ.

Questions for Individual or Group Study

1. In order to make the good news relevant, we need to understand the people we are communicating with—what their world is like and what they think is important. Reread the lists of generalizations about today's adults (pp. 23-25). How would you change these lists to better describe, in general, non-Christians you actually know?

2. Working with your new, improved list:

   • Place an M next to the characteristics that you possess.

   • Star the attributes that you admire in others.

   • Check off the characteristics that might indicate a person would be open to the gospel.

   • Underline the characteristics that might indicate a person would hesitate to give Christianity a hearing.

   • Place a box next to the characteristics that Christ specifically promised help with. (If you want to, jot down any verses that come to mind.)

3. Of the five categories in question 2, which do you think would be important to keep in mind when presenting the gospel to someone? Why?

4. What types of information would you like to add to your lists? How would it help you reach out to others with the gospel?

5. Because it's easy to *assume* we know people even when we don't, Paul Little suggests we develop listening skills so that non-Christians can speak for themselves. In what situations this week could you get some non-Christians to share their views?

6. The author goes on to say that non-Christians value the opinions of people who are informed about and involved in society. How informed and involved are you?

7. If you think you need to improve in this area, what first step could you make this week?

8. Even though we know we're imperfect, non-Christians expect us to demonstrate what being a Christian can be. However, not every supposed Christian demonstrates a faith worth watching! Review the three types of faith Paul Little describes: *indoctrination faith* (p. 33); *conformity faith* (pp. 33-34); and *commitment faith* (pp. 34-35). Which type of faith do you think you possess? (Expect to find traces of the others as well.)

9. If yours isn't commitment faith, would you like to have this kind of faith? You may need to make a conscious, lifelong decision to belong to Christ. You may need to determine to obey Christ, even when it's difficult. If necessary, talk to a mature Christian to decide what the next step is for you.

10. What will you do this week to deepen your relationship with Jesus Christ?

SUGGESTIONS FOR A STUDY-GROUP LEADER

1. Before your study, choose two *brief* news articles—one

about a community service project and another about a recent crime. As you begin the study, read portions of both to
the group. Ask group members to mention what they think
the articles indicate about our society.

2

The Effective Ambassador

———— 🌿 ————

About once every six months the pressure to witness used to reach explosive levels inside me. Not knowing any better, I would suddenly lunge at someone and spout Scripture verses with a sort of glazed stare in my eye. I honestly didn't expect any response. As soon as my victim indicated lack of interest, I'd begin to edge away with a sigh of relief and breathe the consoling thought, "Everyone who wants to live a godly life in Christ Jesus will be persecuted" (2 Timothy 3:12). But duty done, I'd draw back into my martyr's shell for another six months' hibernation, until the internal pressure again became intolerable and drove me out. It really shocked me when I finally realized that I, not the cross, was offending people. My inept, unwittingly rude, even stupid approach to them was responsible for their rejection of me and the gospel message.

Is that what witnessing is all about? Spouting a lot of Bible verses at non-Christians? Not quite. Witnessing goes far beyond what we say at certain inspired moments. It involves all that we are and do. It's a way of life, the "art" of explaining to someone who Jesus is and why trusting him as Lord and Savior is the best news in the world.

Witnessing is one of the keys to spiritual health. I like to call it the fizz in the Pepsi of the Christian life, because it puts sparkle and verve into our faith. When we tell others about Jesus Christ, we study the Word of God with new eyes to sharpen our ability to communicate its message. We pray to God in specific name-address-phone-number terms for our friends in whose lives we are involved. We ask God to illumine them specifically, to introduce them to the Savior and a new life. With anticipation we watch God answer prayer. We will see indifference or antagonism ebb and interest grow. Meanwhile, the Bible becomes increasingly alive when we see others respond to its truth. Passages that once seemed dry and extraneous take on new meaning. When we see the Holy Spirit transform the life of another, we will know we are on the cutting edge of supernaturalism. We can relate not only our own story of God's work but also the updated events of God's work in the lives of others. Our faith index will skyrocket.

Witnessing is that deep-seated conviction that the greatest favor I can do for others is to introduce them to Jesus Christ. "We, then, are ambassadors for Christ." This is the figure the New Testament uses to describe our role as witnesses. We are God's representatives, appointed to be his messengers. God actually makes his appeal to the world through us Christians (2 Corinthians 5:18-21). Imagine being an ambassador for the foreign policy of the kingdom of heaven! It's a tremendous appointment, when you think through its implications.

In a very real sense we are God's only mouth, his only feet, his only hands. When the apostle Paul said we are ambassadors, he was addressing the entire church in Corinth, not just a select few. As soon as we are born into the family of God through trust in Jesus Christ, we automatically receive this commission to give out Christ's message.

Paul went on to tell the Corinthians what the message is to be: that the God of all the universe offers reconciliation to our world. He describes it in three ways: it is the ministry of reconciliation (v. 18), the word of reconciliation (v. 19) and a call to be reconciled to God (v. 20). He is saying that our whole world has walked away from the living God and that it needs to come back. And a loving God stands with his arms wide open, waiting for us to come. What a message for us to bring to a lonely world! What a challenge for us!

Have you ever really considered—that you are Jesus Christ to the people you know? You and I are his instruments standing in the place of the Lord Jesus Christ, beseeching others to be reconciled to God. To me that is a grabber. As you and I go to work, walk down the street, talk to our roommates, visit over the back fence, we are face to face in conversation with people for whom Christ died. We may even be the last link in the chain that stretches out to them from the throne of God, the chain God forged to bring them to faith. There may be no one else they know who can tell them God's message of reconciliation. And that carries with it a solemn responsibility. The privilege of it as well, it seems to me, is overwhelming.

THE ENTHUSIASTIC AMBASSADOR

One of the primary requisites for effective ambassadors in the political realm is that they be enthusiastic about what it is they represent. In other words, they need high motivation. Suppose you were choosing ambassadors to send overseas to represent the United States. You would certainly choose the most qualified people and you would avoid those who think the U.S. is hopeless and who couldn't wait to leave it for good. Ambassadors like that would never make it. Rather, you would want people who may see all of the country's problems but nevertheless are proud to be Americans and are convinced that representing the United States is a great privilege.

In the same way, if we rightly understand it, ambassadors for the foreign policy of the kingdom of heaven need the intense conviction that our message is the greatest gift imaginable— better than a million dollars, better than a cure for cancer, better than anything you can think about. Without this kind of enthusiasm, we won't make it as Christian ambassadors.

What I am talking about is a deep-seated conviction that comes from the depths of our being. It's that sure knowledge that the Christian message is the greatest gift we can give because of what Jesus Christ has meant in our own lives. This kind of inner drive will spur us on to effective and fruitful ambassadorship.

Now let me clarify. When I describe enthusiasm and motivation as ambassadors for Jesus Christ, I'm not talking about a hollow, vapid kind of whipped-up, artificial enthusiasm. It's not beating the chest, saying, "I'm happy, happy, happy," because that's the Christian party line. Nor is it putting on a plastic smile regardless of how we feel.

Not Total Perfection—Not Gabriel's Twin

On the contrary, our prayer should always be that the quality of our lives will honor Jesus Christ. Our sense of spiritual purpose in life, the values we hold, the things that consume our energies should convey a positive witness. Attitudes of quiet peace and contentment that uphold us in life's pressures can speak of God's help.

I'm not suggesting that we should wait for moral perfection before we represent Christ. This is one of Satan's favorite lies. He wants to keep us quiet by convincing us that we mustn't witness to anyone about Jesus Christ until we're good enough to pass for the angel Gabriel's twin. After all, we mustn't be hypocrites. Unfortunately, this lie has worked in countless lives.

Openly sharing our own struggles and the help Jesus Christ has given us in specific situations can produce a thirst in the hearts of those who have never met Jesus. Struggles are different from willful, persistent rebellion against the Lord. Rebellion is outright defiance of the Lord, such as telling the Lord you'll go your own way and for him please not to interfere. Struggles, on the other hand, stem from wrestling with temptations which everyone experiences. These come to all of us in the process of developing maturity, Christian wholeness and likeness to Jesus Christ. This kind of honesty and reality can help non-Christians see the nuts and bolts of the Christian life and the supernatural power we have available to us.

The reality we share with others is the daily, open fellowship we have with Jesus Christ. The personal weaknesses and failures we feel most keenly are often not seen by people who don't know Jesus Christ. The message we have to tell is that daily fellowship with Jesus Christ through the Holy Spirit reveals our sin and that Jesus willingly forgives us when we sincerely repent. Then the Lord Jesus gives us his impeccable righteousness. If this is what we communicate, non-Christians will see the life of the Lord Jesus himself reflected in us.

But we must never forget that though we may be different from other people, we are not perfect. If our message becomes our perfection, we are untrue to the message of Jesus Christ. Besides that, there is nothing that turns non-Christians away faster than the unspoken attitude, "I'm perfect and you ain't!" That attitude contradicts the Christian message. We represent, not our own perfection, but the perfection of the Lord Jesus himself.

As D. T. Niles put it, "Christianity is one beggar telling another beggar where to find food." All of us fall short of the maturity that the Lord Jesus desires of us, and we must freely admit it. The one time to keep silent, in my opinion, is if I have deliberately turned to sin and disobedience and have cut off my own contact with the Lord.

Sometimes the question is asked, "Which is more important in representing Christ—the life I live or the words I say?" This question throws the consistency of our lives and our verbal witness into a false antithesis. It's like asking which wing of an airplane is more important, the right or the left! Obviously both are essential; likewise life and lip are inseparable to an effective witness for Christ.

Normally witnessing grows out of a life commitment to Jesus Christ, and our friends should sense through their pores some eternal dimension when they know us. This is the meaning of Matthew 5:16, "Let your light shine before men, that they may see your good deeds and praise your Father in heaven."

Now *light,* it seems to me, is the gospel and communicating it in words. Our *good deeds* are our personal validation of that gospel. If we were simply silent, hoping people are going to see Jesus Christ, they may only think, "Those are really nice people." It would be like a cancer victim learning about a cure before any other patient knew about it. After he is cured, he would return to the ward, run up and down, do handsprings, cartwheels and handstands. He thinks, *I'm going to be a silent witness about the cancer cure.* If he only demonstrates his health, no one else would get cured. He's got to tell them where to get the treatment. The Scripture teaches that both the verbal message and our living for Jesus Christ are important.

NO FORTRESS MENTALITY

They would be poor ambassadors indeed who went overseas only to build compounds around themselves and their fellow diplomats and never venture forth to meet the citizens of their host countries. In the same way, it would be sad for us to build fortresses around ourselves and befriend only believers. The solution, of course, is to get out there and meet people!

Our lack of opportunity to deliver our message often comes because we have little contact with non-Christians. Both as individuals and in our Christian groups (churches and otherwise), non-Christians are not hearing our message. They are not within the sound of our voices! The gospel hasn't lost its power, but Christians have, in fact, lost their audience. If we don't know any non-Christians, how can we introduce them to the Savior? This simple point explains a lot of the apparent powerlessness of the gospel in today's world.

There are essentially two kinds of opportunities to witness that we have naturally. The first kind is the "one-time" opportunity, such as brief times on a plane, bus or train when we chat with people we've never met before and will probably never see again. Although these conversations are brief, they can get very personal and deep, perhaps because of the anonymity. The people we meet will never see us again, and we don't know anyone they know. Then there are the chance encounters in a doctor's office, at the health club or in a shopping mall. Wherever there might be a conversation that gets started along general lines, we may turn it into a time to talk about Jesus Christ. These may not be "reaping" times, as the New Testament calls them, but they can be significant "sowing" times.

The other kind of contact is with those we see repeatedly— our families, roommates, lab partners, neighbors, business colleagues. These are doubtless the larger number of our social contacts. While it would seem that this continuing group is our primary witnessing responsibility, they are often the most intimidating. We clam up most with those we know the best. We wouldn't think of saying something to them that they might consider outlandish—we have to live with them. Besides, they know all our faults. How can we say anything "spiritual" to them? On the other hand, with a stranger whom we'll probably never see again, we can be really bold. Nevertheless, in both of these kinds of relationships we are God's ambassadors, appointed to declare his message of reconciliation.

We would think it odd if the American ambassadors merely put a sign outside the embassy compound stating, "If you want to know about America, knock. We're waiting inside to answer your questions." Yet many churches and Christian groups run on that principle. Some of us hold evangelistic meetings with few or no non-Christians present.

Even though some non-Christians do venture into our churches, there are even more outside. At an all-university campus lecture series, I saw a clear example of the need to go to the people. Several hundred students turned out for each of the evening lectures in the large university auditorium. That was wonderful. But we saw the need to schedule meetings in the living units—the sororities, fraternities and dormitories. When we did, an additional thirteen hundred non-Christian students heard the gospel message at the smaller meetings! Very few of these students in the smaller groups could have been persuaded to attend the main lectures. But in their own units, they listened willingly. And some of them became Christians. We still value the lectures and need to use many approaches to win others for the Lord. But the fact remains that we often reach significant numbers when we go out to meet them on their own ground.

NOT ALL EXTROVERTS

When it comes to social encounters, there are generally two kinds of people in the world, the extroverts and the introverts. The extroverts may not need any reminders how to meet people and develop friendships. They do it naturally. And God can wonderfully use this gift in setting up social situations. In groups and individually, they easily establish rapport with new people.

Introverts, on the other hand, may need to develop further interpersonal skills. But that does not mean introverts are not attractive to others. They are—especially to other introverts. Their quiet nature often makes them appear more approachable to equally quiet persons. Sometimes outgoing persons come on too strong.

You may find it easier to strike up a friendship with people with personalities and dispositions similar to yours. Outgoing persons build friendships more quickly with others who are also outgoing. More intellectual or philosophical types find more common ground with others of their type. Fortunately, God made us just as he wants us, with unique talents. He has persons for each of us to reach out to and touch in our own particular God-given styles. He would have us all be ambassadors.

Four guidelines for relating to others have been helpful to me:

- *Establish good eye contact.*

Do you look people in the eye or do you tend to stray to north, east, south or west and not center? The eye conveys the soul's intention. A cold eye distances you from others. A warm eye draws you closer. Ask a good friend to tell you honestly if you have warm eye contact.

- *Develop good listening skills.*

Do you focus your attention on what other people are saying? Or are you thinking only of what you are going to say next? And are you genuinely interested in understanding what they are saying? Does it matter to you? If you listen attentively, they will come closer to you.

- *Foster an attitude of encouragement.*

Are your responses more likely to be negative than positive to other people's ideas? Do you put people down? Are you always looking for ways to appear smarter or more knowledgeable than others? Or do others feel warm and affirmed when they are with you? Don't be a negative Nelly or a nasty Nathan!

- *Make yourself interesting to others.*

Many Christians have nothing to do with non-Christians because they would not know what to say if left alone with them for half an hour in a social situation. They have become so removed from the mainstream of life that they have lost touch with how to relate on matters other than religion. One well-known Bible teacher told me he wouldn't know what to say if he went to a Kiwanis Club meeting. If this is our problem, a good knowledge of current events and significant books can give us common ground socially. Developing some hobbies and finding ways to share them with others is helpful too. This may mean learning how to run with a partner, taking up racquetball or simply learning how to explain your interest in astronomy or computers in a way that will interest others.

Three helpful books on the subject of establishing and maintaining good relationships are *Making Friends* by Em Griffin (InterVarsity Press), *The Human Connection* by Martin Bolt and David G. Myers (InterVarsity Press), and *Friendship* by Don Posterski (Project Teen, Canada). Posterski's book offers many insights into today's youth.

A TRUE DIPLOMAT

If we are serious about representing Christ, we need to think through how we can be the best friends possible to non-Christians. It takes effort for all of us to resist socializing exclusively with our Christian friends (or Christian cliques). After all, we rationalize, the Christians understand our background, our vocabulary and our value systems. It's easier! There's no risk.

Instead, ask the Lord to make you more aware of those you rub elbows with every day and see who might need a friend. Perhaps it is the person who lives next door to you, either in your dorm or in your neighborhood. Be specific about who you might begin with. Don't retreat into some kind of impersonal approach. (Well, I'll send them a tract or a book.) It may mean simply spending an hour visiting the person in the next room in your dorm or chatting over the back fence of your home or asking someone in the office to have lunch with you. But be specific because realistically, making new friends may need to be scheduled. Then pray.

Mealtime is always an excellent vehicle for socializing. It is interesting to consider the number of times Jesus ate with people whom he wanted to reach. Zacchaeus, Levi and Simon come to mind, and there are many others. But even people who are watching their caloric intake can set up social occasions. Be creative. Pray for God's insight and blessing.

Perhaps you don't know many non-Christians. In that case you may need to plan new activities or go to new places to enlarge your contacts. One man I know goes to the health club regularly for the sole purpose of making friends. The university campus offers dozens of opportunities to reach out. Students might join the choral society, intramural sports, student newspaper or some other campus organization that fits in with their personal interests and abilities. As we participate in campus life, we will be contributing to it positively, learning ourselves and also having natural contacts with non-Christians.

We mustn't forget about the international students on our own or other campuses either; though they have so much to offer, most of them are all alone. Even the most gregarious feel lost and bewildered by our casual, yet fast-moving pace of living. (One student told us the first menu he saw in the U.S. listed *hot dog*. He knew what *hot* meant and what *dog* meant and decided he didn't want American food.) Each friend from abroad needs companionship and understanding as he adjusts to his stay here. We have known some who have become top leaders in their own governments after graduation. And we can have the privilege of getting to know these gifted people and being their friends.

Our own neighborhoods are often the most neglected places for witness. We drive out of our garages without even thinking of what might be going on behind the lace curtains next door. Then we make our way across town to spend time with our Christian friends. Think of your home as a place for friendship, an oasis to offer to someone who needs refreshing. There is no doubt that most non-Christians will walk into our homes ten times faster than they'll come to our churches.

In the initial stages, you might be soundly rebuffed even for a casual friendship. In the first home our family lived in, we prayed systematically for the neighbors on each side of us. We were sure God had put us in that house to be close friends and ambassadors to these two families. We may have appeared overly eager, for as time went on, we saw only superficial friendship with them. Were we failing? we wondered. However, during the same time, we got to know a family around the corner because we carpooled our children to school. They became our close friends. Then we met another family several blocks away who told us their son asked questions about God that they couldn't answer. We took this opportunity to suggest a Bible study together. The study started in our home, and then it rotated to other homes.

From that time on we knew we needed to go around the corner, so to speak, to find someone in whom God's Spirit was working. It was almost like ringing doorbells to see if anyone was home. Sometimes just a brief reference to God would bring a response we could build on. If there was no response, we didn't sink in despair, but kept seeking for someone else around the corner. Not that we drop those who don't respond; we just don't wait forever hoping for a response where there is none.

One thing we've tried in our neighborhood with some success is to host open houses. The best time for us has been from three to five o'clock on Sunday afternoons. We have delivered simple invitations to each home on our block and served plenty of refreshments. A good number usually came and sometimes stayed and talked until eight or nine at night. In our conversations, we freely expressed to everyone that we like to know those who live close by. After that it was easy to get together again with one or two families alone to get better acquainted. Through such activities, as time went on, we would feel free to discuss all kinds of things as any friends would do. Of course, that eventually included our faith.

One family next door to us in our present home became our close friends. We discovered the mother was curious about the Bible and came to our church's Bible study for couples. After about two months, at the close of a study, she expressed with great emotion that she needed to be forgiven. We all prayed together and were deeply moved by the evident work of the Holy Spirit. And we saw the Lord bring peace to her life. That night on the way home we said very little to each other, but the following week my wife got a letter from her. In words that we will always prize she said, "Thank you for introducing me to Jesus. And I didn't even know who I was looking for." The family has now been transferred, and as far as we know her husband is still standing on the sidelines, watching. But we are still close friends.

Each of us should ask ourselves, *Are there people for whom I am praying by name every day, asking God the Holy Spirit to open* their eyes, enlighten them, and bend their wills until they receive Jesus Christ as Lord and Savior? Are there any people with whom I am building bridges and seeking opportunities to show the love of Christ? Am I willing to take further initiative to communicate the gospel to them as the Spirit gives opportunity? If we discover an absence of vital contact with non-Christians, we may simply ask God to show us even one person whom he wants us to befriend, pray for, love and eventually bring to the Savior, and he will show us that one. "Open your eyes and look . . ." Jesus says (John 4:35).

QUESTIONS FOR INDIVIDUAL OR GROUP STUDY

1. Can you think of a time when you—not Christ's claims—offended someone to whom you were witnessing? What insights (from your life or this book) have pointed out the difference now? Given the chance, how would you do it over?

2. When, if ever, have you sensed you were "God's only mouth, his only feet, his only hands" (pp. 46-47) in a situation?

3. Believing we are God's only workers can spur us to action. But taking this too far can turn us into exhausted Elijahs, saying, "I have been very zealous for the LORD. . . . I am the only one left" (1 Kings 19:10). In light of Galatians 6:2, when should you recruit other Christians to help share the load?

4. Paul Little says, "Ambassadors for the foreign policy of the kingdom of heaven need the intense conviction that our message is the greatest gift imaginable—better than a million dollars, better than a cure for cancer, better than anything you can think about." If you think Christ is the best

gift, why? How does this viewpoint affect the way you respond to others?

5. If you think other gifts are more important, why? What would it take to convince you Christ is better?

6. Should "good witnesses" try to hide their faults and doubts, or should they be vulnerable before non-Christians? If you were still searching for Christ, which kind of witness would appeal to you?

7. How important do you think the following friendship skills are: (1) good eye contact; (2) good listening skills; (3) ability to encourage others; (4) being interesting and enjoyable to be with? Honestly rate yourself in these four areas. (Consider asking someone else to rate you as well.) Are there ways you could improve? How?

8. Do you see non-Christians as potential friends or simply as people God wants you to tell about him? With how many non-Christians do you have mutually beneficial relationships?

9. If you need to give yourself the opportunity to meet some non-Christians or know them better, list two to five potential friends and some activities you might do together. Contact at least one of them this week.

SUGGESTIONS FOR A STUDY-GROUP LEADER

1. Allow group members to share how they applied last week's study. You may want to discuss why they succeeded or failed to carry out their personal applications.

2. Have the group role-play offensive witnessing and then courteous witnessing.

3

How to Witness

———— ✤ ————

If we are genuinely enthusiastic about our Lord and are comfortable in making friends, we may naively assume that all our witnessing problems will disappear. However, our real-life experiences show us otherwise. There are times when we try to witness, eagerly expecting a great response, and plunk, we fall flat on our faces. The head of steam we've built up pushes us to deliver our message to the first person we meet. But it comes off as clumsy and awkward. And we lumber away feeling as unnerved as an elephant on ice! On top of that, the unsuspecting victim of our rude attack (which it can often be) makes a mental note to steer clear of us in the future. Or, at the minimum, run at the least hint of a discussion of religion.

As for us, we groan in defeat, "I don't want to see that person again, ever." Then and there we decide to retire from our short-lived ministry of personal witness and settle for a spot behind the scenes. "I'll stuff envelopes and lick stamps," we volunteer. "And if you want me to, I'll even put up posters and pass out hymnbooks. But someone else can talk to people about Jesus Christ. Like Bruce—he has a natural gift of gab."

To pinpoint the problem, we can see that many of us need to learn how to communicate Christ's offer of reconciliation in a clear, attractive way.

FOLLOW JESUS' EXAMPLE

Fortunately (and by the grace of God), a model has been provided for us—all we need to do is follow it. As Peter reminds us, the Lord guides us by his own example (1 Peter 2:21). We can turn and "follow in his steps" in all aspects of our lives, witnessing included. Beyond that, this commission to represent him is a supernatural work empowered by his divine Holy Spirit. We are not in this alone!

As we view the entire life of our Lord, we can learn many things from his encounters with individuals about witnessing and relating to people. Above all, we see his untiring concern that others hear his message. But let's focus on Jesus' interview with the woman at the well in Sychar, Samaria, told in John 4. We can discover some basic, practical principles to follow as we try to represent him. From there, I hope we can consider how we might apply these principles. For the first principle, let's see how he began.

1. CONTACT OTHERS SOCIALLY

The Pharisees heard that Jesus was gaining and baptizing more disciples than John, although in fact it was not Jesus who baptized, but his disciples. When the Lord learned of this, he left Judea and went back once more to Galilee.

Now he had to go through Samaria. So he came to a town in Samaria called Sychar, near the plot of ground Jacob had given to his son Joseph. Jacob's well was there, and Jesus, tired as he was from the journey, sat down by the well. It was about the sixth hour.

When a Samaritan woman came to draw water . . . (John 4:1-7)

The first principle is one we covered in chapter two: we must have social contact with non-Christians. Our Lord sat down at the well in the town of Sychar in Samaria, a place where he would have face-to-face contact with non-Christians. He was not enclosed in a bubble, surrounded by bodyguards. He was in the middle of traffic, so to speak.

With the woman at the well and with other people, we see Jesus taking clear-cut initiative to get close to someone. He "noticed" a tax gatherer sitting at his desk, headed straight for him and said, "Follow me" (Luke 5:27-28). When some of the self-righteous Pharisees saw this they were really incensed. Jesus actually went out of his way to associate with sinful people. In effect they said, "Just look at the kind of people he's talking to—and even eating with! Why he's a friend of tax collectors and sinners!" But he answered them (catch that irony in his voice!), "It is not the healthy who need a doctor, but the sick. I have not come to call the righteous, but sinners to repentance" (Luke 5:31-32).

Dr. Raymond Bakke, the urbanologist, points out that for his day Jesus did a most remarkable thing when he was in Samaria. In John 4:39-41, he talked with a number of Samaritans from Sychar who knew the woman and at their urging stayed with them for two days! He gladly met the woman's friends and acquaintances. Besides that, he must have slept in their beds, eaten their food, talked to them far into the night. This would be like an Israeli today staying with the PLO. It was unthinkable! But Jesus always broke barriers; he refused to consider what mere tradition said. These people mattered to him. They weren't just a few more statistics. Verse 41 puts it, "Because of his words many more became believers."

A great example of this is Dr. Bakke himself. He and his wife moved from the suburbs where they had been studying to the Chicago inner city to live and raise their family there. For twenty years they have worked with and loved the people they live close to. I have no doubt that this is the only way the message of faith and hope in Jesus could penetrate Chicago's dense inner city.

To contact others socially we may need to go out of our usual path, altering our own plans as Jesus did with the Samaritans. What's more, it may take this to break down barriers. But what better way to express the love of Jesus Christ and demonstrate how much we value others?

2. Establish Common Ground

The second principle builds on the first. We must take the time to establish common ground as a bridge for communication.

We Christians tend to pooh-pooh anything that calls for much time and preliminary preparation. We like to skip the "nonessentials" and get right to the point. Preludes are a waste of time, or so we think. Let's give them the message, we insist impatiently. However, most people resent being trapped in a one-way conversation by those who move in and expound their favorite theme without even bothering to find out if their listeners are interested. We would resent it too. High pressure makes us question whether people care about us as individuals or whether we are just a project to them.

We've all been the "victim" of people who only want to hear themselves give their favorite speech. One friend came into my study and saw a file marked "Christian Work." Now he kids me (jokingly, I hope) about whether I have a folder with his name on it. We laugh about it together, but he has in times past met people who made him feel like a Christian obligation that he was working off. Use sensitivity "mixed with grace," as the Scripture says.

Jesus was a master at relating to others. Were he here today he would certainly decry the oddballism we have seen in some power-hungry, money-grabbing Christian celebrities. Flamboyant behavior may attract curiosity momentarily, but it both gives a caricature of true Christianity and discourages serious consideration of its message. Jesus did not call us to be oddballs.

The public display of an erroneous picture of Christianity can be our opportunity to start a good discussion. We can decry this kind of untrue picture and go on to explain who Jesus really was and what he came for. We cannot, in any case, let these poor representatives of Jesus Christ defeat us. We need to foster a positive description that will prompt individuals to probe deeper and discover what Christianity is all about.

Let's look further at the passage.

> When a Samaritan woman came to draw water, Jesus said to her, "Will you give me a drink?" (His disciples had gone into the town to buy food.) (John 4:7-8)

If I had been Jesus Christ, Lord of the universe, I probably would have blurted out to the woman at the very beginning,

"Lady, do you know who I am?" But Jesus didn't approach her that way. He began by making a request. Would she draw him some water?

Notice the woman's reaction:

> "You are a Jew and I am a Samaritan woman. How can you ask me for a drink?" (For the Jews do not associate with Samaritans.) (v. 9)

This request for a drink doesn't seem very dramatic until we see the whole picture. The mere fact that Jesus spoke to this woman at all was highly unusual. By this simple act he demolished social, religious and racial-political barriers. As a man he spoke to her, a woman. As a Rabbi he spoke to her, an immoral woman. As a Jew he spoke to her, a Samaritan. Thus he startled her. While she couldn't quite grasp the significance of his words, she could sense a deeper dimension in his life. He refused to discriminate against her. He accepted her. This is lifestyle evangelism personified.

For this woman, Jesus' mere request was a treasured compliment. It put them on common ground. In the same way, bridge-building with our acquaintances must have a mutuality about it. Sometimes your friendship may start when you ask your neighbor's help or advice. One close friend chides me with, "I don't always want to be a helpee; let me help you." Any friendship must be a two-way street of mutual give and take. It may mean actively seeking opportunities to show love by running errands, helping with a yard project, baby-sitting—and allowing the other person to do the same for you. Our society overvalues self-sufficiency. By allowing others to do for you, you are telling them you are willing to let down the defenses, to be vulnerable with them. This will give them the option of doing the same with you, perhaps about spiritual matters.

Can't you see Jesus with his water gourd in hand, directing the conversation first to this known interest, the water in the well, and then to a spiritual reality about which the woman knew nothing?

He did all this by means of questions. Jesus was a pro at asking effective questions. (It's a skill we would do well to learn.) In his conversation with a lawyer, Jesus began by asking, "What is written in the Law? . . . How do you read it?" (Luke 10:26). He got the man talking. Another time when the Pharisees challenged him about paying taxes, he took a coin in his hand and asked, "Whose portrait is this [on the coin]?" (Matthew 22:20). To the rich ruler who wanted to know how to get eternal life, Jesus asked, "Why do you call me good?" (Luke 18:19). He drew people out with questions, listened to their answers and then gently gave them his message.

I've found it helps to use questions to express genuine interest in people. What's more, if I have trouble getting to know people, I try to get out of myself (stop thinking of myself) and think of what may be going on in their lives. A question will often bring that out. Before long, I find out all kinds of things about them and we are deep in conversation. I learn what makes them tick! Generally speaking, they will open up if our questions stem from genuine interest. As instruments in God's hands, we can positively and patiently begin first where their interests lie. Later on we can profitably discuss spiritual matters together.

Sometimes common ground isn't as easy to come by. My wife and I developed a close friendship with a couple who expressed strong negative feelings about Christianity and especially Christian workers. As we got to know them, we also discovered they had a wealth of information about flowers and the history of our town (they had lived in that town since childhood). Although horticulture is not my purple passion in life—far from it—we learned a great deal from them. We took all our questions about gardening to them, and my wife and I listened and learned a lot about gardening and about our town as well. Gradually, we established a reciprocal interest in one another.

When I would return from a trip, these neighbors would often greet me with questions: "What were you doing at the University of So-and-So? What did you say to the students? Were they really interested?" As I answered, I was able to share with them the power and provision of Jesus Christ for each person. It thrilled us to watch their interest grow. When the Billy Graham Crusade came to Chicago, our neighbors asked if they might go along with us to an evening service. I had a secret feeling that if we had invited them first, they might have resented it and refused to go. We had tried to listen long enough to be sensitive to where they were in their spiritual journey before we even brought up Jesus Christ. And all those hours talking about flowers were very worthwhile because the process built a trust between us. And without that trust there can be no real relationships and very little effective witnessing.

3. Arouse Interest

As we read on in John 4, we find ourselves asking, "How did the Lord Jesus so perfectly arouse the woman's interest and turn the conversation to his message?" He was plainly in control of the situation. Let's read further.

Jesus answered her, "If you knew the gift of God and who it is that asks you for a drink, you would have asked him and he would have given you living water."

"Sir," the woman said, "you have nothing to draw with and the well is deep. Where can you get this living water? Are you greater than our father Jacob, who gave us the well and drank from it himself, as did also his sons and his flocks and herds?"

Jesus answered, "Everyone who drinks this water will be thirsty again, but whoever drinks the water I give him will never thirst. Indeed, the water I give him will become in him a spring of water welling up to eternal life."

The woman said to him, "Sir, give me this water so that I won't get thirsty and have to keep coming here to draw water." (John 4:10-15)

It is fascinating to see this woman's curiosity kindled and begin to burn as Jesus drew her along. His treatment of her certainly contributed to the very positive response she had to him and his message of truth.

In following our Lord's example, we can turn small events in our relationships to a conversation about spiritual things. A neighbor said to my nephew and his wife, "I've been watching your family and your three young girls, and I like what I see coming out of your house." They took this opportunity to talk about some guidelines the Bible gives for family living. Seemingly small things can open doors for a verbal witness.

It is possible to learn how to be assertive, tasteful speakers for the Lord without being obnoxious. To get started, we can buzz the landing field with some words that could direct the conversation and see if there is any response. Jesus did this when he teased the Samaritan woman into asking a question. He mentioned thirst and she responded immediately.

Once the non-Christian takes the first step in showing some response to us, it takes the pressure off of us. Then we can pick up the conversation later with simple phrases like, "I was thinking about the conversation we had yesterday . . ." or "Something I read reminded me about what you said yesterday . . ." or "What were you thinking when you said . . . yesterday?" There would be no pressure or embarrassment in raising the subject again. On the other hand, if we are forcing the person against increasing resistance, we tend to do far more harm than good. Remember how Jesus gently led the conversation.

We cannot create spiritual interest in others' lives, even though we might like to. Only the Holy Spirit can do this. However, we can be instruments in his hand to uncover the interest that he has put there. We will discover there are people who are interested in spiritual reality; we don't have to force ourselves on those who are not interested. It is an enormous relief when we discover that we can legitimately drop the subject when there is obviously no response.

Relieved of the tension of forced conversation with an unwilling listener, we can bring up the subject later. Confident of the Lord's guidance, we will be natural as we introduce spiritual things. In our witnessing we ought to be as relaxed in our tone of voice and demeanor as we are when we're discussing last night's ball game, a physics assignment, a small boy's exploits or our next vacations.

All the people I know who have been used of God in personal evangelism have *expected* to discover interested people. In any group of people or in conversation with any particular individual, they ask themselves, "Lord, is this one in whom you are working?" Then, as the Spirit gives opportunity, they proceed to test the waters.

4. GET THE BALL ROLLING

The question is, how do we get the ball rolling? Jesus did it by making a cryptic statement that precipitated a question from the Samaritan woman. His statement related to her primary needs and at the same time suggested his ability and willingness to meet those needs.

> Jesus answered her, "If you knew the gift of God and who it is that asks you for a drink, you would have asked him and he would have given you living water."
>
> "Sir," the woman said, "you have nothing to draw with and the well is deep. Where can you get this living water? Are you greater than our father Jacob?" (John 4:10-12)

We can begin witnessing by either making a statement or by asking a leading question. Jesus started by mentioning "the gift of God." He also anticipated the woman's reactions. Her questions did not catch him off guard even once. To take full advantage of each opportunity, we also need to consider beforehand the likely responses. As we think about possible situations, let's think through how to get the ball rolling and how to handle these responses.

After even a vague reference to "religion" in a conversation, many Christians have used this practical series of three questions to draw out latent spiritual interest:

- *"By the way, are you interested in spiritual things?"*

Some will answer yes. But even if the people say no, we can still proceed.

• *"What do you think a real Christian is?"*

Wanting to hear people's opinions invariably pleases them. From their responses we'll also gain a more accurate—and even shocking—understanding of their thinking as non-Christians. Besides, they'll be much more ready to listen to us because we have listened to them. Answers to this question usually revolve around some external action—going to church, reading the Bible, praying, tithing, being baptized.

After such an answer we can agree that real Christians usually *do* these things, but we can then point out that that's not what real Christians *are*. Real Christians relate to Jesus Christ as a living person. Then real Christians will want to *do* the things just mentioned. If the non-Christian continues to indicate interest as we explain this, we can still go on.

• *"Would you like to become a real Christian now?"*

An amazing number of people today are drifting in a spiritual fog, yearning for someone to lead them into spiritual certainty. It is common for the discussion to turn to going to church or even being raised in a church. This is the opportunity to say, "You have probably found the same thing is true in your church as in mine; some people who go there know Jesus Christ personally, some do not. Church membership in any denomination does not, in itself, guarantee really knowing God." This gives us opportunity to discuss the difference between a religious background, or even a religious attitude, and knowing Jesus Christ personally.

If we're on the ball, we can seize many other opportunities

to throw out a leading comment. But we frequently lose out in the "art of repartee" by thinking of the appropriate comment an hour later! So plan ahead for those common remarks in everyday conversation that can easily be spoken for the Lord.

Another means of getting the ball rolling is to be alert for opportunities to share about our spiritual experiences. As we get close to people as friends, they will begin to confide in us about their burdens, longings, aspirations, frustrations and emptiness. As they tell us these things, we can say quietly (if our experience was similar), "You know, I used to feel like that until I had an experience that completely changed my outlook on life. Would you like me to tell you about it?" By making a cryptic statement and offering rather than forcing our experience on them, we prevent others from feeling that we're just unloading unsolicited goods at their doorsteps. If they ask to hear about our experience, we should be ready to speak briefly, emphasizing the reality of Christ to us today and eliminating boring and probably irrelevant details. We should simply say what Christ means to us now.

Suppose our experience cannot parallel the ones described to us by our non-Christian friends. What do we say? We know Christ is a reality to us today, so we can say, "You know, I would feel that way except for an experience that changed my outlook on life. Would you like me to tell you about it?"

Those of us who have grown up in Christian homes and churches often develop an inferiority complex because we can't point to a dramatic change in our lives when we became Christians. We can't say, "Once I was a dope addict, but see what Christ has done for me!" If we came to new life in Christ as a child, we probably did not notice much change in our lives.

We need not feel inferior or apologetic about this, as though somehow our experience were not as genuine as the more spectacular. Paul's conversion was wonderfully dramatic, but we must always remember that Timothy's was just as real. From early childhood he heard the Word of God from his grandmother, Lois, and his mother, Eunice (2 Timothy 1:5). The great question for us is whether Jesus Christ really is a dynamic Lord to us today.

There are passages in people's lives that draw their attention to religion and give us wide-open opportunities to get the ball rolling. For students, academic failure, disappointment in love or concern about career choices may open the door. For young couples, the birth of a first child may turn their thoughts to religious training. As families grow, teenage problems can cause the parents to despair. Physical problems, emotional turmoil and financial reverses bring special fears. Divorces are particularly traumatic. We can use any one of these situations to bring up the need for God. When our neighbor phoned and said her husband had had a heart attack, I prayed with her on the phone. My wife brought the family supper. Since then I've given her a book to read.

One woman called our home because she wanted to know if she should build a new house or stay in the old one. When my wife talked to her, she told her that in a very difficult time in her life Jesus Christ had given her peace and wisdom. This woman, obviously prepared by the Holy Spirit, responded, "I want that. I want that." The next day we sat in our family room and read Bible passages to her and talked with her. She literally pleaded with us to help her commit her life to Jesus Christ. Not everyone is so eager and ready; she was moved and made a commitment to the Lord who would guide her in all of her life choices. I can still remember the joy we felt reading to her, "Greater love has no one than this, that he [Jesus] lay down his life for his friends" (John 15:13).

Again, we may be talking about a question relating to church or some religious activity. If we handle it properly, we can arouse interest in the gospel. A question I'm often asked when I'm traveling is, "What kind of work do you do?" I used to reply matter-of-factly, "I'm a staff member for InterVarsity Christian Fellowship." That answer took the conversation nowhere.

Then someone suggested to me that answers describing activity or function always tell more than a mouthful of proper names and titles. So now I explain my work instead: "I talk to students about how Jesus Christ relates to everyday life." This is more likely to bring the response, "That sounds interesting." "It is," I say. "Just the other night I was talking to a student who said . . ." and I briefly give the gist of an actual conversation. Then I ask, "By the way, are you interested in spiritual things?" And the conversation is off and running.

In a discussion about the day's headlines, the latest world crisis or some other current event, the query "What do you think is wrong with the world?" may be appropriate. After listening while various external causes are blamed for mankind's problems, we can say, "I've gotten help from what Jesus Christ said about this." At times like this, if the person is still interested, I try to refer to Jesus' diagnosis of human nature (alienated from God) in Mark 7:21-23. People themselves, because of their inner attitudes, are the basic problem. As G. K. Chesterton aptly put it, "What is wrong with the world? I'm wrong with the world." And the only solution to the "I" problem is Jesus Christ, who has promised to give us a new life and a new purpose for life.

Books and booklets on provocative subjects provide another possibility for stimulating conversation on spiritual matters. One family near us had three rambunctious boys, ages three, four and five. They were always talking about the difficulties they struggled with in rearing their children. One day I loaned them two books on child-rearing written from a Christian perspective. After that I had no problem discussing Jesus Christ with them.

We've also had some interesting conversations that started with friends browsing among the books we have in our living room. We have an array of secular books of various kinds and some special Christian books. We encourage people to borrow them. It gives us the opening to say, "I'd be interested in your reaction to this one." As a rule when I travel, I carry two booklets with me. Two good ones are *Christianity for the Open-Minded* by Michael Cassidy and *Becoming a Christian* by John R. W. Stott (InterVarsity Press). After any conversation, I might offer one of them, saying, "This little book has helped me; would you like to have it?" If it is a one-time conversation, it at least leaves some further information for the person to consider.

Sometimes we can get the ball rolling by inviting people to a small group Bible study at home or in church. If the atmosphere is low key and non-threatening, I've found good response from people who are thinking about God, or even from those who may be lonely and would welcome an intimate group of any kind. It can be an excellent vehicle for making the facts about Jesus Christ clear.

There are two basic things that make such a group effective. The first is an atmosphere that does not make beginners feel either like targets or children who know nothing. If the group is a discussion group, this usually helps. Then people can express their doubts and questions freely. The second thing is to have a definite plan for the subject matter to be studied, including a specific time frame. For beginners, sometimes just a six-week study is attractive. Or a study in the book of Mark for sixteen weeks. In such studies I have often seen complete agnostics change to roundly affirm the facts of Jesus' claims. Then over coffee their personal commitment can be talked out.

Other group events, such as music concerts or Christian films, help the person get the feel of a group of Christians together. A vital group of turned-on Christians can open the coldest hearts. What's more, wherever possible, we want inquirers to eventually join other believers when they commit themselves to the Lord. We're not looking for decisions only; we're praying for people who will wholeheartedly follow Jesus Christ and grow into mature Christians.

In these and similar situations, having a few things in mind to say beforehand will help overcome our nervousness. If we clutch, others clutch; but if we relax, they relax. Any tendency to be apologetic about our faith is easily detected. When we assume people lack interest, we tend to defeat ourselves before we start. On the other hand, if we assume interest we are more likely to get a positive response. As we gain in quiet confidence, the Holy Spirit will lead us to interested people. Each successful encounter with a non-Christian will lead us to greater faith and confidence for the next one.

5. DON'T GO TOO FAR

The next part of our Lord's conversation reveals principles five and six: Give people only as much of the message as they are ready for, and don't condemn them.

Jesus answered, "Everyone who drinks this water will be thirsty again, but whoever drinks the water I give him will never thirst. Indeed, the water I give him will become in him a spring of water welling up to eternal life."

The woman said to him, "Sir, give me this water so that I won't get thirsty and have to keep coming here to draw water."

He told her, "Go, call your husband and come back."

"I have no husband," she replied.

Jesus said to her, "You are right when you say you have no husband. The fact is, you have had five husbands, and the man you now have is not your husband. What you have just said is quite true."

"Sir," the woman said, "I can see that you are a prophet." (John 4:13-19)

Despite the woman's obvious interest and curiosity, Jesus didn't give her the whole story at once. Gradually, as she was ready for more, he revealed more about himself. Then, when her curiosity had reached fever pitch (v. 26), he identified himself as the long-awaited Messiah.

The moment we detect a faint glimmer of interest in non-Christians, many of us want to rush right in and rattle off the whole gospel without coming up for air or waiting for any audience response. (After all, we might not get another chance, we think!) But by relying on the power and presence of the Holy Spirit, we can gain poise. Non-Christians need gentle coaxing when they're just beginning to show interest: it's usually fragile at first. Otherwise, like birds scared from their perches by a sudden movement toward them, they will withdraw. On the other hand, if we are casual in our attitude and relaxed in our manner, the inquirers might even press us to share with them.

Along with this, in your explanation of the Christian faith, start by finding out what basic things you can agree on. Do they really believe in God? What do they think God is like? Is he out to "get" them? Who do they think Jesus is? Do they have any favorite passages of the Bible? Don't assume that they're totally ignorant. Search for a basis to build on. Affirm these things roundly where you can. In my early days, I zoomed in at the start with the idea of correcting. That is, correcting their theology. "Hey, let me tell you what's wrong with universalism!" Just my know-it-all attitude was a turnoff. Nobody listens to a know-it-all.

Regardless of how many people we meet, generally speaking they fall into one of two groups. Those in the first group lack information about Jesus Christ and wouldn't know how to become a Christian if they wanted to. The second group of people have all the information necessary and need only respond to that information. With this latter group, it doesn't help to thump them with the gospel every time we see them. Once we're satisfied in our minds that certain persons fully understand the gospel, it is usually best to drop the subject until they introduce it. In the meantime, we must not separate ourselves from them in any way but continue to love them and pray earnestly that they come into the kingdom of God.

I had a young friend who had come with us to Bible studies for a while and read a couple of Christian books. He had a good grasp of the Christian message. One night we went to a Christian film together and afterward went out for coffee. It was evident that the Spirit of God had touched him, but I could sense that his old wall of resistance was still there. This time, I decided not to talk about Jesus Christ with him unless he brought up the subject. Finally he burst out with some heat in his voice, "I'm not going to become a Christian, you know!" The only response I could think of was, "That's your choice." He already had all the information he needed; now the choice was his. I had a clear sense that it would have been useless for me to continue to press for any commitment.

It is helpful to remember that comprehending spiritual truth is no small thing. Just to grasp the idea of God becoming a man is a mind-wrenching, profound exercise in thought. Let the divine truths sink deeply into the mind and heart of your friends. It may take considerable time. In our church there is a mature woman who is a relatively recent Christian but has grown like wildfire and teaches Bible classes. She often tells how she didn't really grasp how much of a sinner she was until six months after her conversion. Go slowly, and let the Spirit lead.

6. Don't Condemn

In the sixth principle we see that Jesus Christ did not condemn the woman. As she answered his query about her husband, her sin itself condemned her. He didn't bypass the question about her husbands, but he did no finger-pointing or head-wagging in judgment. In another similar incident with a woman caught in adultery who was brought to Jesus, he said to her pointedly, "Neither do I condemn you. . . . Go now and leave your life of sin" (John 8:11). Most of us in either of these situations would have been quick to condemn. It's probably because we have the mistaken idea that if we do not condemn a certain attitude or deed, we will be condoning it. But this was not our Lord's way.

Christians cannot be unmoved in the presence of sin that

clearly separates from God and is self-destructive. This sin is what brought Jesus Christ here to earth to give his life! We must express pain and sorrow. There is no way to be joyful when we are confronted with destructive sin. The rub comes when we feel personally revolted by the filth of sin but want to love the person. Pain and warmth can be expressed at the same time. Sternness and warmth cannot. I am awed by the picture of the divine, holy Son of God standing in front of an exceedingly sinful woman expressing love and forgiveness. "I don't condemn you; there is forgiveness. There is a better way!" Joy and encouragement comes when we turn from sin ("go and sin no more") and are bathed in that forgiveness.

Although we may never have been caught in obvious sins as these women were, our own need for forgiveness must never be forgotten. Our message is never that we are good and moral and we want everyone else to be good like us. We can never discuss another's sin without putting ourselves in the same position of needing help and forgiveness. What's more, we can never let our own less flagrant sins cease to revolt us while we openly are horrified with someone else's more obvious evil. Even the apostle Paul often stated that he was the grossest of sinners.

A good rule to follow in all of our relationships is the simple quip, "You catch more flies with honey than vinegar." Not only must we avoid condemning people, we need to learn the art of legitimate compliment. Many people are deeply touched by a genuine compliment. Criticism sometimes can be far more natural to our lips than praise, but praise can make others more open to the gospel.

In his book *Taking Men Alive,* Charles Trumbull asserts that we can discover in any person at least one thing worthy of an honest compliment. To prove his point he describes one of his own experiences on a train. A cursing, drunken man staggered into his car. After lurching into the seat beside Mr. Trumbull, he offered him a swallow from his flask. Mr. Trumbull inwardly recoiled from the man. But instead of blasting the man about his condition he replied, "No thank you, but I can see you are a very generous man." The man's eyes lit up despite his drunken stupor, and the two men began to talk. That day the man heard Christ's claims. He was deeply touched, and later he came to the Savior.

7. Stick with the Main Issue

As the interview between our Lord and the Samaritan woman draws to a close, we note two final principles that apply to our witnessing conversations:

> "Our fathers worshiped on this mountain, but you Jews claim that the place where we must worship is in Jerusalem."
>
> Jesus declared, "Believe me, woman, a time is coming when you will worship the Father neither on this mountain nor in Jerusalem. You Samaritans worship what you do not know; we worship what we do know, for salvation is from the Jews. Yet a time is coming and has now come when the true worshipers will worship the Father in spirit and truth, for they are the kind of worshipers the Father seeks. God is spirit, and his worshipers must worship in spirit and in truth."
>
> The woman said, "I know that Messiah" (called Christ) "is coming. When he comes, he will explain everything to us."
>
> Then Jesus declared, "I who speak to you am he." (John 4:20-26)

Our Lord did not allow any secondary questions to sidetrack him from the main issue. The woman asked where she should worship, on Mount Gerizim or in Jerusalem, but Jesus steered the discussion back to himself by shifting the emphasis from *where* to *how* one worships.

Though the woman's question was probably valid, our Lord refused to go off on a tangent. Her attitude was similar to the current honest question that many people have, "Which church should I join?" Or we might be asked about hypocrites in the church, errors in the Bible, why are there so many denominations and a multitude of other questions. Any legitimate question can be a tangent if it sidetracks us from the main issue. Jesus left no doubt about the main issue: himself.

The central message of reconciliation must never be left out of our witness. When we are confronted with people involved in especially repulsive acts, call to mind how the Lord Jesus approached the woman in Samaria. And remember his attitude toward the two men, Levi and Zacchaeus, both of them tax cheats. When men and women of all kinds meet Jesus Christ, their lives are changed. Ken Medema's song about Zacchaeus closes in one beautiful line with the message we want to convey: "And so he came, and transformation was his aim."

8. Confront the Person Directly

And finally, in declaring to the Samaritan woman that he was the Messiah, Jesus reached the crucial point of his message to her: "I who speak to you am he." Likewise, whether we spend one or many sessions with friends building bridges of friendship, we must eventually cross this bridge and bring the non-Christians into a direct confrontation with the Lord Jesus so that they realize their personal responsibility to decide for or against him.

Effective ambassadors must know how to invite a decision about the message they are communicating. Now there are a number of people who know how to build the bridges of friendship, take initiative in conversation and get across the message, but they are completely flummoxed when it comes to helping people across the line. How do you find out whether people are ready without being too abrupt? The simple answer is, you ask them! How do we ask them?

For a period of time I used to say to people "Are you a Christian?" but I discovered that wasn't the best way to go about it for several reasons. In the first place, a great many people would say yes, thinking they knew what being a Christian was all about. Soon I was quite sure in the light of the New Testament that they weren't Christians. But once you get a yes answer to that question, you have a problem. You can't say, "I'm sorry, friend. You're all wrong for the following reasons." Somehow they don't appreciate that kind of thing. People have a right to believe anything they choose to believe, but they don't have the right to redefine Christianity. Only Jesus Christ has the right and authority to state the terms of Christianity.

A series of questions I learned from Leith Samuel from Southampton, England, when he was here lecturing years ago, have been worth their weight in gold to me. Here they are:

- *"Have you ever personally trusted Jesus Christ or are you still on the way?"*

Immediately, this question defines clearly what a Christian is and beyond that it lets the person know that you're prepared for a negative response without being shocked. It is very common to have a person respond with, "You know, that's exactly how you describe me. I'm still on the way."

- *"That's interesting. How far along the way are you?"*

This second question follows up the first one and draws people out more fully. It's absolutely amazing how often I have had people explain to me, without the slightest hesitation or embarrassment, how far down the road of their spiritual pilgrimage they are. And that's tremendously valuable information to have. Once we hear them tell us where they are, we can fill in any gaps they may need. Our objective, of course, is to find out where people are and try to help them down the road a bit further.

- *"Would you like to become a real Christian and be sure of it?"*

I proceed to this third question if people indicate any response and frequently they will. Again let me emphasize the amazing number of people who are just waiting to be asked, who are longing for spiritual certainty, but no one has ever told them how to get it. So perhaps you can say to people that you've witnessed to and had some discussions with, "By the way, have you ever personally trusted Christ, or are you still on the way? How far along the way are you? Would you like to become a real Christian and be sure of it?"

These, then, are our eight principles: meet and know non-Christians personally; establish a mutual interest in conversation; arouse a person's interest by life and word; gear explanations to people's receptiveness and readiness for more; accept and even compliment rather than condemn; stay on the track; and persevere to the destination. Once we begin to grasp these principles and move out in faith, life becomes a daily fascination. We watch with anticipation to see the next opportunities God will give us to bear witness as ambassadors of Jesus Christ and to discover how he is working in the lives of others through us.

Questions for Individual or Group Study

1. Paul Little points out that Jesus' contact with the Samaritans was as radical as an Israeli camping out with the PLO. In fact, Jesus' whole attitude toward the Samaritans makes it hard for us to believe they were hated by the Jews. What gave Jesus the ability to treat the Samaritan woman with such respect? In Luke 10:25-37, 17:11-19 and John 4:4-42, how did Jesus show his respect and liking for these people?

2. According to this chapter and your own experience, how can we show non-Christians respect and appreciation?

3. The author mentions a time when non-Christians asked what made "the difference" in his nephew's family. If you're one of the many fine Christians who have *never* had this happen, how do you handle this potential disappointment?

4. In the past, how have you successfully brought up the topic of Christ and his claims? Review this chapter's suggestions for broaching the topic (pp. 71-77). Which of these might work for you?

5. Christians often have a chance to share our spiritual experiences when others ask our advice. The problem for us is knowing what to say! Take some time to think of two or three instances when knowing Christ helped you with a problem or fear. Think through how you would share these with a non-Christian (emphasizing Christ's reality today, omitting unnecessary details, and so forth).

6. Paul Little allows Christian literature to be his partner in

witnessing. Do you have any Christian booklets, books, magazines, articles or albums that you think a non-Christian might appreciate? Is there anyone who might like to borrow your copy now?

7. This chapter suggests inviting non-Christians to Christ-centered events (Bible studies, concerts, films). Is there a way you could do this in the near future?

8. The author says it's easy to tell non-Christians more than they are ready for or want to hear. How can we avoid this costly error?

9. This chapter ends with a caution: It's destructive to condemn or set ourselves up as better than others. How can we help others see themselves realistically before God without condemning them?

10. Paul Little offers eight principles for witnessing: contact others socially; establish common ground; arouse interest; throw out the bait; don't go too far; don't condemn. What would you add to his list?

SUGGESTIONS FOR A STUDY-GROUP LEADER

1. Allow group members to share how they applied last week's study. You may want to discuss why they succeeded or failed to carry out their personal applications.

2. Consider pairing off the group so pairs can role-play asking and answering the questions, "What do you think a real Christian is?" and "Would you like to become a real Christian now?" Have pairs share with the larger group what they learn from this exercise.

4

Hurdling Social Barriers

———— ❧ ————

Anyone who moves out of the safety zone of a Christian group and gets into the real world is sure to run into ticklish situations. We need to consider beforehand how we may cope with some of them, working out principles that will apply in varying circumstances.

USE THE CASUAL TOUCH

How, for instance, should we react to profanity or filth? Perhaps we think the godly thing to do is swish Victorian skirts around us, in a holier-than-thou attitude, complete with scathing remarks or icy silence. When we react like this toward the crowd in the office or dorm, it merely serves to distance us from them. They're only doing what comes naturally for them and criticizing them can rob us of the chance to build friendships with them. If we grow huffy whenever people swear, they may start dredging up every profane expression they've heard in the last two years, just to get our goat. We've intensified the problem we were trying to solve.

Dr. D. Martyn Lloyd-Jones, in his study on the Sermon on the Mount, makes this point, "To expect Christian conduct from a person who is not born again is heresy. The appeals of the gospel in terms of conduct and ethics and morality are always based on the assumption that the people to whom the injunctions are addressed are Christian."

The message of an ambassador for Christ is first and foremost to be a witness to a God who reconciles. It follows then to ask yourself this question: Will I get that message over by acting as a school marm out to correct everyone's behavior? Or, will I be starting at the wrong end of God's truth? Always keep in mind that it is God, not us, who transforms hearts and behaviors. And he begins on the inside.

I've known two men who had what I would consider pretty crude vocabulary. The one not only swears up a storm, but his attitude is usually close to belligerent. For some reason he appears to take great delight in acting as gross as possible whenever we're together. I usually feel he's trying his best to put me down. If he talks to me directly I can count on him to be brusque and abrupt. I've made up my mind to refuse to play his game, which would be to get annoyed with him. (That is what he would really like, I'm convinced.) Besides that, I know he has a lot of deep, unresolved hurts inside and is stubbornly fighting any thought of giving his life to Jesus Christ. In situations like this, the Christian can maintain their own self-respect and not blast back. It means resisting the drive to react emotionally toward the person.

I know another man, a bit younger than the first one, who when we first met used similarly raunchy language. He came to a small group Bible study, openly eager to learn. No one said anything about his vocabulary, mainly because we could see he was so obviously absorbed in learning. Sometimes he swore during the discussion, but it didn't seem to matter. He was soaking up all we were saying. Gradually, in a wonderful way, we saw the Lord Jesus transform that man. He became a witness and a leader, and he developed a new vocabulary as genuine and pure as his character. We all learned to look beyond the externals to the intention of that person. It made us more understanding witnesses.

Whether someone is Christian or not, it is axiomatic that we cannot change other people's behavior. In the light of this, if we are going to influence anyone for Jesus Christ, it pays to use the casual touch. Don't hit people with a sledge hammer! That only serves to dull their hearing.

THE AMBASSADOR'S GOAL

Our guideline for a right attitude in hurdling social barriers should be the ambassador's goal: to get close enough to gain a hearing for the message of reconciliation through Jesus Christ.

We see this single-mindedness over and over again in the life of our Lord Jesus. Note how he controlled the conversation with Nicodemus until he could spell out for him the new birth (John 3:1-5). When he healed the paralytic man, he refused to be cowed by the skeptics that watched. He took the discussion right where he wanted it: "That you may know that the Son of Man has authority on earth to forgive sins" (Luke 5:24). This was what they needed to know, and he wouldn't be deflected from it. In another instance he faced the opposition from disbelieving Jews with total aplomb, a man in charge of himself and the situation. These Jewish religionists finally got the point that he was claiming to be from heaven, and they were dead set on disproving it. Jesus waited until they had their say and then went straight to the core, "I tell you the truth, he who believes has everlasting life. I am the bread of life" (John 6:47-48). There are dozens of other illustrations of this; resolutely, Jesus kept his eye on the goal.

We get sidetracked easily when we make a particular behavior pattern a part of being a Christian. Suppose we consider drinking alcohol out of bounds for us. Down deep we know it's right to be up front about who we are and what an ambassador for Jesus Christ is all about. When an invitation comes to take a drink, we're caught off guard, and reflexively reply, "No, thank you. I don't drink; I'm a Christian" or some such thing. The iron gate clangs down between us and the other person. The person pulls away as if we're poison and we can see we've lost the chance to build any kind of bridge of friendship. Is that a witness? What we've really done by implication is condemn the person, by implying: "You're not a Christian, you drink!" No wonder the person backs off.

More importantly, we've made this particular "don't" an inherent part of Christianity, and Christianity is unequivocally not what we "don't" do; it is "whom" we trust. Giving this kind of reply doesn't help make our message clear.

Thousands of non-Christians within our culture have very strict moral codes and would agree with all of our behavior patterns. Obviously, that doesn't make them Christians. At the same time, in some cultures Christians do drink and think nothing of it. They are none the less Christians. Custom and personal conviction determine some of these habits. Now, if a friend suggested, "Let's go rob a bank," and we said, "No thanks, I'm a Christian," he would clearly understand the connection. The eighth commandment distinctly forbids stealing. There is no other way for the Christian to interpret "Thou shalt not steal."

There is a good guideline I've followed that helps me in situations like this. It is: Do not condemn the other person and do not compromise your own convictions. I've also come up with some ways to help me accomplish that goal.

Use Substitution

When we receive invitations from people whose personal customs and convictions differ from ours, the key is to recognize the compliment and the generosity implicit in the offer or invitation and then decline on a personal preference basis. In that way, the person doesn't feel condemned or rejected. One way to say "No thanks" is to suggest an alternative activity. If we're asked to go somewhere we'd rather not, we could respond, "Thanks! I'm not interested in that, but let me know when you're going to a game (or concert, club meeting, whatever), and I'll go with you." By suggesting an alternative possibility the person doesn't feel rejected personally.

If non-Christians aren't interested in playing chess, they don't blush, hem and haw, and finally mumble apologetically, "No thanks, I don't play chess. I'm a non-Christian." Of course not. They reply breezily, "No thanks, I don't really like chess. But let me know when you want to play tennis." As witnesses for Jesus Christ we can and should say "No thanks" in this same easy, unembarrassed spirit.

In the biography of his son Sandy, Leighton Ford tells how Sandy got caught in this different-lifestyle dilemma. When he and another student were praying about meeting other students, they were invited to a PJ party (short for pajama, of course). The problem was, PJ was also a mixture of punch and liquor and the sole purpose of the party was to drink as much as possible as fast as possible. Picture Christians in the middle of that! Well, they really wanted to be ambassadors to these students and decided God wanted them to go. They put their robes on over their jeans and just as everyone else was carrying their PJ or beer, they took their six-packs of Pepsi. Because they jauntily substituted their own brand, the crowd fully accepted them and the other students made the six-packs of Pepsi their trademarks.

One man I know who's in the business world merely states when he's offered liquor, "Thanks, but I'm nonalcoholic." Or one could merely say, "No, thanks, but do you have 7-Up?" If we have a forthright plan for our style and a confident attitude, others will accept it and us. In all we do, good humor and enjoyment should characterize a developing relationship.

HAVE A GOOD JOKE READY

Speaking of humor, it is not uncommon to find ourselves in an escalating conversation that is getting more and more bawdy as our comfort level gets lower and lower. If we could, we'd like to just walk away, but we're caught and can't excuse ourselves. In situations like this, our best course is positive preparation. Be alert for the first lull in the conversation, and then jump in with a good clean story. Tell one so funny that people can't help laughing. Some people think I'm joking when I say this, but I'm not. I'm convinced that all Christians should have five sure-fire jokes at their disposal. Well-chosen, well-timed humor can reset the whole tone of a conversation; it can carry you over a seemingly impossible hurdle.

Remembering jokes is like remembering names. As soon as you hear one, use it. If necessary, write it down; then tell it whenever you get a chance.

Contrary to a popular belief, Christians don't have to give up their sense of humor when they become Christians. Some people have stereotyped Christians to resemble the cartoon of the church group that was meeting their new pastor at the train station. When they approached a man they thought was the pastor coming off the train, the man said, "I'm not your new minister. I just have a stomachache." Take heart; we can correct this impression. We may not indulge in the same kind of humor as others, but we can be spontaneous and find laughter and zest in everyday life. Moreover, we know there is wholesome humor and delight in living every day for Jesus Christ.

BEGIN NOW—WHERE YOU ARE

Right now someone's probably thinking, "Boy, this sounds good, but I would need to start over, go some place where no one knows me. Then I could make a go of it. But the mess I've made I can't redeem. Who can unscramble an egg?" If you feel this way, don't give up. No situation is a lost cause. On your part, things can be transformed.

I know a young woman who resolved before God to make a new beginning right where she was. She'd been working in the same office for eight and a half years. Every noon hour while the rest of the office staff ate lunch together, she sat alone in a back room to eat by herself. She couldn't join in some of the stories and jokes her coworkers told but didn't know how to be positive in that kind of atmosphere. Finally, though, she decided to just be a friend to a few. Motivated by love for the other women, she searched out a couple of funny stories of her own and began to mix with the other women at lunch. Six months after her first weak-kneed but joke-supplied attempt, she told me that the other women seemed genuinely happy that she joined them. She had even witnessed to two of them. It's true! Changes can come right where you are.

Giving Thanks in Public

Another secondary issue that warrants some thought is the whole matter of giving thanks before a meal. When we're alone in a restaurant, we should have no question about bowing our heads to give thanks. But what about when we're out with a group or at a business lunch? When the awkward moment arrives, our natural reaction is to want to pray, but we conceal it. We fumble with our napkins or clear our throats and hope for two seconds of silence so we can pray and start to eat before the meal gets cold. The waitress, if she's looking, must wonder if we have a headache or are smelling the food. Giving thanks can be embarrassing! One of my Christian friends brought me up short one day in a restaurant. "Shall we scratch our eyebrows?" he asked, and caught me with my hand in midair. We had a good laugh, but I learned my lesson too. Before then I'd never realized how enslaved I was to finding some diversionary tactic.

Check out to see if your way of saying grace offends or implies to another person, "You're a pagan; you don't give thanks." To avoid creating this barrier to friendship, it may be best for us to keep our eyes open while we thank God for our food. No verse of Scripture dictates "Thou shalt say grace with thine eyes closed." God looks at our motivation and our hearts. In any case, I think we would all agree that the sole purpose for giving thanks is our gratitude toward God. It is not a witness vehicle! If I know my companion well I sometimes casually say, "It's my custom to give thanks for my food. Would you like me to say grace for both of us?" In the right situation, this is not usually an affront.

ENTERTAINING GUESTS AT HOME

When we entertain in our homes, the situation is a bit different. There's no question that when we have guests, we should do what is customary for us. A simple word of explanation before-hand will prepare our guests. Something like, "It's our custom to give thanks for our food before we eat, so I'll just pray for a moment." If our guests aren't religious, and we don't explain our custom, they may be unnerved by our ritual. It's only courteous to tell them what we're about to do. The same principle applies if we have Bible reading and prayer after dinner. As we have said before, be relaxed and natural. And above all, courteous.

A broader aspect of our social involvement with new friends is the whole question of inviting them into our homes for a visit. To begin with, we may think, *We don't have anything in common with non-Christians,* and then we're stymied. Suppose we can find nothing at all that interests us both and the visit turns into a flop. Maybe they'll be bored if they join us in something we like or maybe we'll be embarrassed if they suggest we go some-where with them.

This dilemma is easily solved by planning what we'll do to-gether beforehand. Instead of just saying, "Joe, can you come over Tuesday evening?" or "Several students are coming over for

the weekend. Can you come?" we can make a specific suggestion to play table tennis or to go skiing. This solves the problem
at the outset. People know what to expect and if they're not interested they can decline the invitation without embarrassing
anyone. Or they might suggest an alternative activity you all will
enjoy. But nine times out of ten, they'll want to come.

Don't Necessarily Follow the Crowd

Some of our associations are in groups formed by our circumstances, not by our choice. It may be at work or in a civic group
or in a dorm situation, but we feel a certain amount of peer pressure to be like everyone else in the group. Usually, in such cases,
our behavior can be different than the rest of the members without anyone taking it personally. Consequently, one-on-one
relationships can be developed even though we choose to buck
the crowd on some activity.

Going to college throws us into group life, such as living in
a dorm or Greek house twenty-four hours a day with non-
Christians. The same is true if we have a stint in the service with
Uncle Sam. Before we enter any group situation, but especially
one of considerable duration, it's good to determine ahead of
time what habits we're going to keep. Then keep them from the
beginning. If you usually give thanks for your food, remember
to say grace at the first meal. If you have a daily quiet time, include it in your schedule the very first day. You set the pace. If
you don't establish your pattern at the outset, each day you put
it off will make it harder to begin later on.

You may find yourself in a group that has developed wonderful feelings of fun and camaraderie, even some conversation
about the Lord. And then someone pulls out a joint or puts a

porn movie on the VCR, or someone starts making sexual advances to you. The pressure you feel may make all the resolutions you've made in the past seem inappropriate. These are friends you see all the time. They're a part of your life. What are they going to think if you suddenly get "picky" on them?

This time, substitution will not work. Bluntly, there is only one thing to do. Move! Get out of the place as soon as possible. But get out graciously. Try something like, "Hey, I'll take a pass on this. See you later." It's not necessary to make a judgmental statement that will forever cut off your contact with the friends. The only thing you need to be clear about is your own involvement. Remember Daniel. He made a clear statement to the chief of the eunuchs to allow him not to defile himself (Daniel 1:8). In any group, whether by action or words, God's children must be unambivalent about who they are. Keep in mind too that God blessed Daniel and his three friends so they were "ten times better than all the magicians and enchanters" (Daniel 1:20).

Most of the time there is opportunity beforehand to make a choice about whether to join in a group activity. If we know we'll be unfaithful to our Lord if we go along with their plans, we can simply bow out graciously. Without beating around the bush we could say, "I'm not into that—but if you wind up doing something else, let me know." Or you might feel better with, "You go ahead. I think I'll stay home and watch TV." Although most people today are floating downstream, they respect the few who are fighting against the current. In private conversations they'll even admit their admiration; they wish they had the courage of their convictions too. Someone who's inner-directed rather than other-directed stands out! Others will also respect us if, while we have the courage of our convictions, we don't arbitrarily legislate others' choices for them.

There are times when your options for action are limited. To the Christian students living in dorm rooms day after day with others whose practices they reject, there may be times when your choices are limited. If possible, try to attempt an agreement on some of the basics for the room. By all means, have an open discussion together on the differences and state preferences unemotionally. (Remember, all negotiations go more smoothly if both parties are calm. This is a good rule for any circumstance.)

There may be things you don't like but in a pinch could live with, such as your roommate's leaving around porn magazines. On the other hand, if your roommate invites an overnight guest of the opposite sex, you have a right to put your foot down on that. This may not help very much if there's an open policy in your school, but you might just find your roommate willing to listen. In such close living quarters, you may find a tension between being humble and being a doormat. Jesus Christ never calls us to give up our moral courage. Keep in mind Daniel's example. We are redeemed children of God!

"In" Vocabulary

We've talked about the vocabulary of those we want to get close to, but we need to examine our own words too—and the walls they can build. Every group has its own set of "in" words that all its members understand. Christians have a veritable mass of them. We use *the Word* when we refer to the Bible, and Christians all know what it means. Or Romans 8:28 conveys a lifetime of meaning for us. Then there are words like *salvation, reconciliation, justification* that we use freely. We talk about "accepting Jesus as our personal Savior" and expect a beginner to comprehend the how and why as we do. And maybe we even lapse into the King James English! The noted linguist Eugene Nida calls this Christian "in" language *Protestant Latin*. It's something like a person who's never owned a computer hearing the buffs talk about the world of *MS-DOS, modems, mainframes, data bases, encryption* and *megabytes*. It's a foreign language and leaves the outsider on the sidelines.

Remember that outsider feeling when you talk about God, Jesus Christ and the Bible. Check yourself carefully. Develop a mind sensitive to the ears of a beginner. Say your thoughts as simply as possible to begin with. Keep your words uncluttered and pause a while to see if the other person is lost. Our insider vocabulary can create its own social barrier.

EXPRESS LOVE

We aren't devising gimmicks to get at people surreptitiously with the gospel when we discuss these potential social barriers. We're genuinely seeking ways to express the love of Jesus Christ effectively. He has come into our lives and given us the capacity to get out of ourselves and love others. It is his love "shed abroad" in our lives that we want to pour out for others. We love people for themselves, as individuals rather than abstractions. If Jesus Christ is a personal reality to us, his love might reach out through us to some very unlikely people whom everyone else might shun. The very capacity to love them comes from him.

The very best expression of our love for others is when we are able to communicate the love of Jesus Christ for them. But no friendship should depend on how the other person responds to the message. Unfortunately, today people in general are justifiably suspicious of all Christians because of the flood of counterfeit, pseudo-examples of followers of Jesus Christ. Or some may have met a friendly religious person who turned out to have ulterior motives and dropped them suddenly when they didn't believe. We may not be able to say a single word to those people about Jesus Christ until they're sure we'll be their friends even if they reject Jesus Christ. We must love people for themselves.

None of us can play God for other people. We can never determine the level of true response to the Holy Spirit in others. It may take several years and a long period of indecision before certain people open their hearts. For Jesus Christ's sake we must continue to love them nonetheless. It is the Holy Spirit, not we, who converts an individual. We, the privileged ambassadors of Jesus Christ, can give the verbal message; we can demonstrate through our personality and life the grace of Jesus Christ. We cannot go around chalking up scalps, taking credit for the Holy Spirit's work and saying, "Wow! I've got seven!" Such spiritual pride is wholly out of character for a follower of Jesus Christ.

The anticipation of an ambassador is the possibility of reaping, of being the last link in a long chain, and seeing people receive Jesus Christ as their Lord and Savior. Should this happen, it does not mean that we have converted souls and brought them to Jesus Christ. If someone says, "I've converted two people!" I think I know what the person means. But I shake my head in amazement. No one truly calls Jesus "Lord" except by the Holy Spirit.

Ours is the incomparable privilege of being ambassadors of Jesus Christ. He has chosen to use us as his only representatives in a lost world that yearns for eternal reality.

Questions for Individual or Group Study

1. Paul Little states we shouldn't expect Christian conduct from non-Christians who don't have the Holy Spirit's guidance and strength. How far would you take this statement? What *should* we expect from them?

2. To make an issue out of people's actions is to start at the wrong end of God's truth. What, instead, should our comments and attitudes convey about Christ and his claims?

3. This chapter suggests the ambassador's goal is to get close enough to gain a hearing of the message of reconciliation through Jesus Christ. Are there ways your attitudes and actions distance others? How?

4. Besides those the author mentioned, are there other social barriers that hinder your communication with non-Christians?

5. Christians often get sidetracked by making a particular behavior pattern part of being a Christian. Did reading this chapter point out any pet do's or don'ts you've been equating with the Ten Commandments? If you're part of a Christian community that has "extended" the Ten Commandments, how will you deal with this?

6. Paul Little's philosophy is: "Do not condemn the other person and do not compromise my own convictions." He suggests substitution, jokes, agreeing ahead on an activity, setting your own standards and casually leaving a group as ways not to compromise. Which have worked for you in the past? What would you add to his list?

7. Many Christians have a hard time being assertive. This may be why we overstate the point when asked to do something we think is wrong. Think through what you could say the

next time someone asks you to go against your conscience.

8. In order to arm yourself with good, clean jokes, you may need to plan ahead. List (or research) five or six jokes, anecdotes or stories you think are funny. *Reader's Digest* is a gold mine. Practice them until you can tell them effectively.

9. You can probably list off the activities you would not feel comfortable doing. Do you have as ready a list of interesting activities you'd enjoy doing? If not, write one now.

10. Occasionally we do compromise our standards. At such times, it's easy to blame our non-Christian influences, thereby doubly condemning them. What would be an alternative response in the situation?

11. Do you speak Protestant Latin around new Christians or non-Christians who may not understand? What might be your motivations for using such in-language? How could you keep from excluding others?

SUGGESTIONS FOR A STUDY-GROUP LEADER

1. Allow group members to share how they applied last week's study. You may want to discuss why they succeeded or failed to carry out their personal applications.

2. Come armed with six or seven funny jokes or anecdotes, perhaps from *Reader's Digest,* to use in introducing question eight.

5

What Is Our Message?

Ambassadors communicate a message. Many Christians are ineffective ambassadors because they're not sure of the content of their message and are unable to communicate it clearly to others.

For many people, understanding the gospel is like understanding a mathematical problem. They hear the math problem explained in class and clearly understand it as the professor goes through it. But when friends who cut the class ask them to explain the problem, they just can't do it clearly enough for their friends to catch on. Many who have believed and understood the gospel for themselves are unable to articulate it clearly enough to others so that they, too, might know and experience the same Lord.

DON'T BURY THE TRUTHS

For other people, they feel they must include many true, but irrelevant, facts in order to fully explain the gospel. The major truths get buried in the weight of facts that are helpful but not central to the gospel. As a consequence, the hearer is confused. Not even the crucial question of whether the Bible is the Word of God should detract from this central message. If we try to answer that question, we may never get to the more important question of who Jesus is. Should the question come up, it usually is enough to show that the Bible is a reliable historical document and on this basis confront the person with the claims of Christ. After trusting the Savior, it is only logical to adopt the position Jesus Christ took toward Scripture—that it is the inspired Word of God.

For a beginning, when we communicate the gospel, it is essential to realize that Christianity is not a philosophy or a way of life but a living person, Jesus Christ. Unless non-Christians see the issue is their personal relationship to this person, we have failed. The confusion about the true, ungarbled definition of Christianity is virtually an epidemic. I actually heard a Christian student tell how he was driving with a non-Christian along the highway in Pennsylvania. They passed a sign that said, "Jesus saves." His companion remarked very sincerely, "That's something I never thought of before. If Jesus is thrifty, I ought to be too!"

The issue is not what church people should belong to, what amusements they should not attend, etc. Here are some of the popular misconceptions of what Christianity is and brief explanations to dispel them:

Christianity is not . . .

- *Being a Gentile.*

There are many Gentiles who would be furious if you called

them Christians, and there are many Jewish people and adherents of other world religions who have become Christians.

- *A heritage.*

One can no more be born a Christian than one can be born married. It has been aptly stated that God has no grandchildren!

- *Going to church.*

An old but true statement is, "Going to church no more makes you a Christian than going into a garage makes you an automobile." Christians do go to church and fellowship with the people of God, but that is not how they became Christians.

- *Participating in a particular ritual.*

Again, this is something real Christians will do, but it is not that which makes them Christians.

- *Following the teachings of Christ.*

Again, those who have been transformed by Christ will follow his teachings and will seek to reflect the moral image of Christ in their lives. If they claim to be Christians and live the way the devil does, the New Testament says they are not Christians and do not have life. However, they cannot enter the presence of God solely on the basis of the life they lived unless they can match the perfection of Jesus Christ. Of course, no one can do that!

- *Adhering to certain negatives.*

The Christian life is a very positive, dynamic thing. What Christians refrain from are actually positive, constructive things to them, but may be seen by others as negatives. The Christian life expands people rather than restricts them.

- *Believing the facts about Jesus Christ.*

We have already seen that mere intellectual assent does not produce Christian life.

WHAT CHRISTIANITY IS . . .

The gospel, then, is Jesus Christ himself—who he is, what he has done and how he can be known in personal experience. Because the gospel is about a person, there is no rigid and rote way to present it. If we are describing a person rather than a formula, we would naturally begin with the aspect that seemed most relevant at that moment, whether it was the person's appearance, character or personality.

If you have a blond brother who is studying chemistry at Harvard and you meet someone who is also studying at Harvard, you wouldn't begin the conversation by saying, "I have a brother who is blond, is studying chemistry and is at Harvard." No, you would begin, "Oh, I have a brother who is at Harvard," and you might then go to other facts as they are relevant. On the other hand, if you meet someone who is almost an identical twin to your brother, you wouldn't begin by saying that you have a brother who is studying chemistry. You'd probably say, "You look just like my brother," and then go on to other facts.

In the same way, when we talk about the Lord Jesus Christ, we may decide his resurrection will grab the person's attention, especially if the person jumps in to contest the deity of Christ. With another person it might be Jesus' death or his diagnosis of human nature or who he is. Eventually, we will want to cover all the information about the Lord Jesus so the person has a full grasp of who he is and what he offers.

For ourselves, our aim is to be conversant with all the basic facts of the gospel that a person ought to know to become a

Christian. And, of course, we'll need to know where these facts are documented in the New Testament.

BASIC FACTS

What are some of these facts? The following is a brief outline. It is by no means exhaustive, but it will at least give a framework for our thinking and some foundations to use for a springboard to present the gospel. Where possible, this outline follows the principle of using our Lord's words and the clearest references to support the facts.

1. Who Is Jesus Christ?

He is fully God. A number of New Testament references document this, but the following are among the most explicit: John 5:18; John 10:10-30; and John 14:9. When we talk about the claims of Christ, it's helpful to use the words of Jesus himself, as there are some people who will accept only his own statements rather than the disciples' statements. Use the phrases that state it most simply. Those verses which involve a prediction or a claim to deity that you may have heard in a Bible class will not be so understandable to the non-Christian. For example, to begin with Genesis 3:15 which talks about the offspring of the woman crushing Satan's heel as referring to Jesus would leave the beginner totally in the dark.

To tell people that Jesus is fully God, we need to keep our radar on in order to sense people's understanding of God. To some people God is a kind old man who wouldn't hurt a flea. To others he's like a high priest with a sharp ruler in his hand. When we say Jesus is God, we are saying that he is eminently trustworthy. He is truth. He is holy. He is Creator and Lord of the universe, and yet we matter to him. He has true, pure love for each of us, his creation.

At the same time it must be stressed that Jesus is fully man (John 4:6; John 11:35). When Jesus was here on earth, he was the ultimate example of a man who knew why he had come to earth. He did what he knew was right, obeyed his Father in heaven and said only the words that the Father had told him. He downplayed himself and was wise and virtuous. He was tempted as any man is tempted, yet he was totally without sin. At the end of his life he died a hideous, undeserved death for the sake of others. This was really a man!

2. His Diagnosis of Human Nature

After considering Jesus Christ, fully God and fully man, we turn the person's attention to Jesus' view of us, his creation. How does he see us? The clear-cut answer is in Mark 7:1-23, where Jesus says that all of us have a basic disease, sin, which defiles us and cuts us off from the holy God who cares about us. This sin has a variety of symptoms and "comes from within a man," as Jesus said in this passage. It originates internally and not externally; we can't blame anything or anyone else for it.

It is helpful to define sin experientially rather than propositionally. Merely to tell someone that "all have sinned" doesn't usually get the biblical idea across. In our society sin is a nebulous, ill-defined thing that has lost any meaning. People have told me it refers to My Sin perfume by Lanvin! Others have said it refers to one specific kind of immorality. If they don't happen to be guilty of this kind of immorality, they become highly incensed because they do not see themselves as sinners in these terms.

However, if we describe sin in experiential terms almost all hearers agree that this includes them. We can begin with an easily recognized fact that we don't have to teach children to sin; it shows up in all of us very early. Who of us has not lied or cheated? Who hasn't been cruel, hateful, jealous, covetous or self-centered? And that's just the beginning of the list!

Any list of overt acts proceeds from the inner disease of the heart which Jesus described. The symptoms vary widely with different people. Its root is the basic disease of rebellion against God, of going our own way rather than his. Of saying to the Creator, I know better than you how to run my life. This root of rebellion is not just for the bum on skid row; we are all in this together. This disease and its results are universal. We are separated from God like a leaf cut off from a stem. Beyond that, it is this separation from God which is at the heart of our boredom, loneliness, moral weakness, lack of purpose and more.

3. The Fact and Meaning of His Crucifixion

Without the sacrificial death of Christ, this would be a hopeless story. We would remain estranged from God, turned only into ourselves. The sequence of events that led to Jesus' crucifixion is described in each of the four Gospels. In Matthew 26:28, our Lord himself gives the reason for his death in one short sentence. He said, his life is given for many "for the forgiveness of sins." In Matthew 20:28, he explains he will "give his life as a ransom for many." Webster defines *ransom* as "obtaining the release of a captive by paying the demanded price."

Peter, who was one of our Lord's closest disciples and hence knew his mind very clearly, states it unambiguously: "For Christ died for sins once for all, the righteous [Jesus] for the unrighteous [the human race], to bring you to God" (1 Peter 3:18). Jesus Christ took the sentence of death that belongs to us because we have all broken God's moral law. He stepped into our place to receive our judgment, and now he freely offers us forgiveness. The result is to restore us to the relationship that God intended for us at creation.

4. The Fact and Meaning of His Resurrection

The dramatic account of Jesus Christ rising from the dead is likewise found in each of the four Gospels. Perhaps the most vivid one is in Luke 24:36-45. After Jesus' death, the disciples returned to the Sea of Galilee to fish. Suddenly Jesus "stood among them and said to them, 'Peace be with you'" (v. 36). You can imagine that they were frightened and thought that they had seen a spirit. But Jesus said to them in those classic words, "Touch me and see; a ghost does not have flesh and bones" (v. 39).

Jesus Christ had risen from the dead! His body was resurrected, not merely his spirit. This single, inarguable fact is the supreme validation of his deity. Moreover, he showed himself by many infallible proofs in ten distinct recorded appearances. It was these appearances of the resurrected Jesus that revolutionized the life of the early Christians. They were frightened and defeated on Good Friday, but after Easter Sunday they launched the mighty Christian movement. For us too the implication of the resurrection is that the Lord Jesus Christ is here today, a living person. He is alive and powerful to invade the life of all who invite him into their lives.

And it is this resurrection power, available today, that makes Christianity unparalleled and unique.

5. Becoming a Christian

We have listed the facts about Jesus Christ—his deity, his death, his resurrection and our separation from him. But these are more than theological facts. They describe every one of us, and require more than a mere nod of the head in response. Indeed, they demand a response that involves a change of mind about how we view sin and a determination to turn to God. The mind must comprehend the holiness of God and our own utter failure and inability to measure up to God's standard of perfection. Paul, in his defense before Agrippa, said he preached that both Jews and Gentiles "should repent and turn to God" (Acts 26:20).

The emotions are also involved in turning to God. "Godly sorrow," in contrast to one's being superficially sorry for sin, often precedes faith in the Lord. In 2 Corinthians 7:10, Paul explains "godly sorrow brings repentance that leads to salvation." Although emotions are no gauge of true repentance, we should be sure to experience some feeling about it.

The final test of true repentance involves the will. The prodigal son not only came to his senses intellectually, but he acted: " 'I will set out and go back to my father.' . . . So he got up and went" (Luke 15:18, 20).

At this point, people need to take that first step of coming to trust Jesus Christ personally. But it is not always easy for us to explain this experience vividly. We use vague, abstract terms like *believe, have faith,* etc., which do not describe concretely what is involved in becoming a Christian.

It seems to me that the clearest statement in the New Testament on how to become a Christian is John 1:12, "To all who received him, to those who believed in his name, he gave the right to become children of God." There are three operative verbs in this statement: *believe, receive, become.* Someone has said that in becoming a Christian there is something to be believed and someone to be received. This aptly sums up this verse.

It is significant that marriage is one of the illustrations the New Testament uses for being and becoming a Christian. It is obvious that merely believing in a man or a woman, however intense that belief might be, does not make one married. If, in addition, we are emotionally involved we still are not married!

A bachelor may say to us, "Sure, I believe in marriage. I'm sold on it. You should see all the books I've read; I'm an expert on the subject. Besides, I've been to plenty of weddings. Funny thing, though—can't quite understand it: marriage doesn't seem real to me." Very simply, what he hasn't discovered is that to become married, a man first believes in a woman and then must receive her into his life. To get married, one finally has to come to a commitment of the will and say, "I do," committing himself to the other person and thereby establishing a relationship. It involves total commitment of intellect, emotions and will.

But while we may smile at this bachelor, some of us may be just like him. The parallel is obvious. People may know all about Jesus, yet not know the Lord himself. Being a Christian requires committing ourselves to a living Lord. This commitment depends on a relationship of love and obedience. We must believe in Jesus, personally receive him into our lives, and thus become children of God.

This analogy illustrates that mere intellectual assent to facts does not make a person a Christian any more than mere intellectual assent to facts makes a person married. Many people's dissatisfaction with Christianity is because they are like the bachelor who stood on the edge, but never jumped into marriage. They may have read a dozen books on Christianity and even taken religion courses, but never made a commitment. It will be obvious to us that marriage is not Philosophy Number 67 as opposed to Singlehood 12. Nor is Christianity Philosophy Number 78 as opposed to Existentialism 3, Agnosticism 14 or Logical Positivism 21. Rather it is a dynamic relationship with a living person, the Lord Jesus Christ. Just as getting married means giving up our independence and living in a consultative relationship with our spouses, so does receiving Christ. The essence of sin is living independently of God—going our own ways rather than his way. So is the essence of non-Christians. They are living independently of God and following their own ways.

The substance of repentance is the repudiation of our self-centered lives and making Christ and his will the center of our lives. When we marry, we must think of another person in all our decisions. When we receive Christ, we enter into a consultative relationship with him about every area of our lives. Our first thought must be: what does he think and desire for me? The beauty of it is that what we do with our lives matters to God.

How then does one actually receive Jesus Christ? In Revelation 3:20 Jesus Christ compares our lives to a house and says, "Here I am! I stand at the door and knock. If anyone hears my voice and opens the door, I will come in and eat with him, and he with me." Showing this verse, I often ask interested students, "Suppose someone came to the door of your room and knocked. How would you get the person inside?" The students think for a moment and then say, "Why, I'd open the door." I say, "Exactly. And then what would you do?" Invariably they respond, "I'd invite the person in." Usually a flash of insight crosses their faces as they realize that this is exactly how one becomes a Christian. The Lord Jesus Christ is knocking at the door of our lives. He will not gatecrash or force his way in but will come in at our invitation. This invitation can be given him simply in our own words in prayer. And when we receive him, he promises to come in and be with us for eternity.

BASIC PATTERN

These five basic facts of the gospel are the foundational truths for us to master so we can explain them easily when the time comes. Rarely can these all be laid out, as such, with people. They are to be our broad, general guidelines. Along with these, we also need a fairly easily understood format to summarize for people. Let me list just a few used by others and me.

1. Three-Phase Pattern

- Jesus' definition of what's wrong with people: They are separated from their Maker (Isaiah 53:6; Romans 3:11-12).

- Jesus' diagnosis: Our disease of sin causes this separation (Mark 7:15).

- Jesus' solution: Restore this relationship through his death (Romans 5:8; 1 Peter 2:24).

2. Four Steps to God

- God: Twin facts—he is holy; he is the loving Creator (1 John 1:5; Psalm 100:3).

- People: Twin tragedies—we have rebelled; we have broken God's law (James 2:10; Psalm 14:2-3).

- Jesus Christ: He reconciled people to their Creator by his death (Romans 5:6-8).
- Required response: Repent, believe, receive (Acts 17:30; John 1:12).

3. Jesus' Definition of Christianity

- "I am the bread of life" (John 6:35).
- "I am the way and the truth and the life" (John 14:6).
- "I am the light of the world" (John 8:12).
- "Come to me" (Matthew 11:28).

4. Religion Versus Christianity

- Some believe Christianity is something you can do—that my good deeds must outweigh my bad deeds. They think, "If God grades on a curve, I'll get in" (Titus 3:5).
- The Bible says: "For it is by grace you have been saved, through faith—and this not from yourselves, it is the gift of God—not by works, so that no one can boast" (Ephesians 2:8-9).
- Christianity is something that has already been *done:* Only Jesus Christ can make us good enough to enter heaven. He forgives our sin and gives us his righteousness (Romans 5:8).
- The Bible says: "For we maintain that a man is justified by faith apart from observing the law" (Romans 3:28); "Therefore, since we have been justified through faith, we have peace with God through our Lord Jesus Christ" (Romans 5:1).

5. Roman Road

- "All have sinned" (Romans 3:23).

- "The gift of God is eternal life" (Romans 6:23).

- "Confess with your mouth . . . believe in your heart" (Romans 10:9-10).

You may have other concise summaries of the basic gospel message to use as your springboard. But whichever method or methods you choose, remember that we live in a biblically illiterate society. Guard against inside language. We will probably be deeply disappointed if we assume that our listeners have biblical knowledge and understanding. It helps to clearly define terms which have great meaning to us but very little meaning to non-Christians, such as, *Christian, Savior, eternal life, sin, born again, regeneration, salvation, saved, propitiation, sanctification, justification.* What do we actually mean by these words? The best way to know is to sit down and write out a definition without using the word itself.

THREE STEPS

I would like to suggest a few practical steps for improving our knowledge and understanding of the message itself.

1. Write out the gospel in letter form.

Direct the letter to a hypothetical friend who has no objections but is ignorant of the gospel. Explain what a person needs to know to become a Christian. Ask someone to read the letter and evaluate it for you. You might even think of someone appropriate to mail it to.

2. With a Christian friend, role-play sharing Christ's message.

Try your role-play twice—the first time your friend should pretend to have little initial interest in spiritual things. Then try again, this time with your friend inquiring about what a Christian believes.

3. Tell a non-Christian friend about your project.

Ask your friend if he or she has time to listen to you explain the content of what a Christian believes. Suggest that you are trying to learn to communicate in an understandable way and would appreciate any help he or she can give. The only guarantee we are communicating plainly is when the other person can say back to you the very thoughts you wanted him or her to know.

FOLLOW-UP

What would you think of a mother who brought child after child into the world but abandoned them each after birth? The same could be said of people who bring others into the kingdom of God and then abandon them to fend for themselves. Caring for young Christians is every bit as important as helping them become children of God. After a new believer decides to trust Christ, the decision needs to be strengthened with an understanding of all of its implications. Not all new Christians have the same needs, but here are some guidelines.

1. Provide the big picture.

New Christians need help understanding the big picture of the gospel. That is to say, they need to know that God is calling all people from the kingdom of darkness into the kingdom of light. Their experience is part of the larger work of God in the whole world. They have heard the call of God as have many other people. Then too they will need help to be able to articulate what has happened to them.

2. Direct them to spiritual food.

They have to quickly learn how to feed their new spiritual lives. "Like newborn babies, crave pure spiritual milk" (1 Peter 2:2). Give them some limited but very specific instruction about reading Scripture. Don't just say, "Go read the Bible." What will they do? Naturally, as with any book, they will start at the beginning. And how many people have you and I met who began to read the Bible in Genesis but collapsed by the middle of Leviticus?

You may want to explain how the Bible is laid out (separate "books" listed in a table of contents in the front, chapters indicated with a large number or the word *chapter* and sentences called *verses* indicated by a small number next to the text). Mention that because the Bible was not originally written in English, it has been translated by different people throughout the years. Different translations have different wording, but the essential message is the same in each version. Offer to help new believers choose a version that will meet their needs.

Suggest that they read the Gospel of Mark. Watch them look it up for themselves and make sure they can locate specific verses, explaining that such skill will come in handy later.

Then perhaps give them one or two questions to answer for themselves as they read the book. They could ask themselves, "What do I learn about the Lord Jesus Christ from this passage?" Next, they could ask, "Is there a command to follow and how will I do it?" There are many other questions you could give them, but *just give them two.* They can experience success doing such a simple, specific assignment, and they can get that wonderful experience of God speaking to them directly. Another possibility is to suggest a small study guide for them to follow.

The booklet *Quiet Times for Christian Growth,* by Kelly James Clark, offers forty quiet-time Bible studies geared toward new Christians on prayer, fellowship, service, evangelism and guidance (InterVarsity Press).

If you can, meet with these people regularly, or phone or correspond with them. If you do not live close by, contact a local church that would be willing to help these new Christians get a strong start in their Christian lives.

3. Offer assurance of salvation based on God's promises in the Bible.

New Christians often need some help with assurance that they are children of God. What's more, they need to know that feelings are not the basis of assurance. Our confidence is based solely on "having the Son," as 1 John 5:11-13 points out. No doubt sinful habits may plague them, as they plague all of us. Let them know that there are some changes that ought to begin to take place in their attitudes and lives. Don't keep assuring people that they're in the family of God if there's no evidence of God's Spirit in their lives. At this point, explain to them patiently and clearly what it means to believe and receive the Lord Jesus Christ.

4. Help them understand how to deal with sin in their lives.

New Christians can be staggered by the fact that sin is still a reality in their lives. They may need you to point out the difference between *fellowship* and *relationship* on the basis of 1 John 1:9. If two married people have some harsh words and feel like breaking up, the situation can look very bad. But when they make up, they don't need to get married all over again. Their relationship is secure. It was established once for all when they got married. But they did have a problem with fellowship and communion, and the only way it's going to be restored is by confession and restoration. It's the same thing in the Christian life. We need to tell new Christians how they can overcome sin in their lives. Show them 1 Corinthians 10:13 and how to look to Christ at every point of temptation.

5. Help them maintain healthy relationships with non-Christians.

After some people become Christians, they seem to sabotage their relationships with the non-Christians closest to them. These relationships suffer a great deal of damage. I've talked to a number of people who have had great heartache—particularly young people, teenagers and students—when they go home to their families. They can be very enthusiastic about becoming Christians, but if they go about sharing their enthusiasm in the wrong way, they can create barriers to the gospel that last for years. The more intimate the relationship, the more delicate it is.

These young people should go home, and before saying anything, start picking up their rooms. Or offer to help around the house. Or stay home a few nights a week. And when the parents wake up from a dead faint, and say "What on earth has happened to you?" then they can tell their stories. 'Well, you know, Mom and Dad, maybe you've known this all your lives, but it's suddenly become meaningful to me." And then tell them what Christ has come to mean to them, without implying that their parents are ignorant heathens.

However, many young people go home and communicate in a variety of ways, "Where have you been for the first years of my life? I now know what it's all about, and you'd better get with it too." Again, these people sincerely want to express what has happened to them, but the hurt that is caused is incalculable. The same care and thoughtfulness should temper people's approach to non-Christian friends.

6. Help them find fellowship.

Finally, it is absolutely crucial that we introduce new Christians to other Christians and to a local church fellowship. The Lord Jesus knew we would need the warmth and support of the family of God. In fact, that's one reason he established the church. Tell new believers that the church is a place of growth in the knowledge of the Lord and in Christian service. These two factors should be their litmus test for choosing a church. If they find they're not growing spiritually and in a knowledge of the Scriptures, they need to pray for guidance about their future relationship with a particular church. Assure them that God will lead them.

Working with new Christians can take time and energy, but the eternal rewards are the greatest available. Ask God to give you a heart for these young believers and to use you to help them develop a lasting commitment to him.

Questions for Individual or Group Study

1. Successfully presenting the gospel is not necessarily having a person accept Christ as Savior. Rather, it is knowing you've clearly and accurately presented Christ's claims and what he demands in order for people to be reconciled with God if they so choose. When you've tried to explain the gospel in the past, did you experience "success"? Why or why not?

2. By answering the following questions, explain the basic facts of the gospel Paul Little presents on pages 108-15.

- Who is Jesus Christ?
- What is his diagnosis of human nature?
- What is the meaning of his crucifixion?
- What is the significance of his resurrection?
- What does it mean to become a Christian?

3. If a non-Christian made the following statements to you, which misconceptions about Christianity would the person hold? How would you answer each?

- "Frankly, I don't see much difference between the way Christians and non-Christians live."
- "I'm already a Christian because I was baptized as a child."
- "I come from a Christian home. I was born a Christian!"
- "I wouldn't want to be a Christian. The Christians tried to exterminate my people, the Jews."
- "I attend the same church Billy Graham does!"

4. Besides the misconceptions Paul Little mentions, have you come up against others that non-Christians believe? How do you handle them?

5. The author suggests that we should begin our presentation of Christ and his claims with the information that would most interest our specific hearer. How would you progress if a person mentioned one of the following statements?

- "I've messed up my life hopelessly."
- "I'd like to find the true religion, but they're all alike, really."
- "I don't think I've ever been loved by anyone."
- "I'll tell you why there is so much suffering in the world! God is out to get us!"

6. What would you reply to a person who said, "I'm glad Christ

will forgive my sins but I haven't got anything to repent of. I'm as good as the next guy"?

7. What responsibility does the "spiritual parent" of a new Christian have to help that person grow in Christ?

8. Compare the Bible with any other book—format, multitude of versions, purpose, how we read it, and so forth. How would you explain this unique book to new Christians so they can use it without being overwhelmed by its thousands of fact-packed pages?

9. Why do new Christians need help relating to their non-Christian families and friends? How would you advise them?

10. Prepared with new insights from this chapter, would you like to contact someone in order to explain or clarify the gospel or to help the person continue in Christ? Consider doing so this week.

Suggestions for a Study-Group Leader

1. Allow group members to share how they applied last week's study. You may want to discuss why they succeeded or failed to carry out their personal applications.

2. Pair off group members. Then use the statements in question five as a basis for role-plays of one person explaining the claims of Christ to another. As a large group, have people share the lessons they learned and the difficulties they encountered in doing this role-play.

3. To introduce question eight, set up role-plays in which one person explains Bible use to someone who has never really looked at a Bible before. (The "new Christian" should demonstrate a realistic ignorance of the book.)

6

Why We Believe

In our time it's not enough to know what we believe as Christians; we must also know why we believe it. All Christians should be able to defend their faith. We're clearly instructed about this spiritual responsibility in 1 Peter 3:15: "In your hearts set apart Christ as Lord. Always be prepared to give an answer to everyone who asks you to give the reason for the hope that you have. But do this with gentleness and respect."

This command is not optional and there are good, practical reasons for it. First, for the sake of our own conviction about the truth, we should have an answer ready. Unless we are fully persuaded in our own minds that Jesus Christ is the truth, we will never effectively communicate the gospel to someone else. Moreover our own spiritual lives will soon become impoverished. We cannot drive ourselves to do with our wills something about which we are not intellectually convinced; the result is emotional collapse. We ourselves must be convinced of the truth.

Second, we have a responsibility to help thoughtful non-Christians deal with their honest questions about Christianity. If we are constantly silenced by non-Christians' questions, we are confirming their reasons for unbelief.

I'm not suggesting we should stop witnessing about Jesus Christ if we don't have all the answers. We can always point to our own experience, as did one courageous man Jesus healed. In John 9, when he was asked questions he couldn't answer, he told his critics simply, "One thing I do know. I was blind but now I see!" (v. 25). When we don't know the answers we can always stand squarely on what we *do* know: Jesus Christ has changed our lives. However, this should not be our only recourse. We are responsible for mastering the answers to repeatedly asked questions.

TWO HARMFUL ATTITUDES

In considering and answering the questions non-Christians ask, we need to avoid two opposite but equally harmful attitudes. The first is basically an anti-intellectual attitude. Some people assert, "You don't have to bother with human wisdom. Don't even try to think out Christianity." They imply that it's wrong to try to work ideas through.

Or you'll hear, "Don't get sidetracked by people's questions. Just preach the simple gospel." The tragic result of accepting such a view is that many thinking non-Christians conclude from our behavior that their honest questions have no answers. And we sometimes begin to wonder ourselves whether or not we have the truth: if we faced the facts as they really are, would our faith hold water? The anti-intellectual attitude is usually a dead-end street for both the non-Christian and for us.

Second, we must guard against a naive reliance on the answers we have, as though answers themselves will bring people to Jesus Christ. Sometimes we think that any explanation that makes sense to us and has helped a few others is a magic wand. We think we'll go out and wow people with it, so they'll have no choice except to believe. Of course, we're naive in thinking this, for we've already noted that no one calls Jesus Lord except by the Holy Spirit. Unless the Holy Spirit illumines people's minds to see the truth as truth, unless he bends their proud wills to submit to the authority of Jesus Christ, no words of ours will penetrate. But in the hands of God an intelligent answer to their questions may well be the instrument that opens their hearts and minds to the gospel.

There is no doubt we are in a spiritual warfare involving ourselves and the questioners. Paul explained the reason that people do not believe: "The god of this age has blinded the minds of unbelievers, so that they cannot see the light of the gospel of the glory of Christ" (2 Corinthians 4:4). Information cannot bring them to the truth unless a supernatural work also occurs to enlighten them. Often God and the Holy Spirit will use a presentation of information as an instrument to bring someone to faith in Jesus Christ.

CATER TO INTELLECTUAL INTEGRITY

John Stott, rector emeritus of All Souls Church, Langham Place, London, struck the proper balance in his statement: "We cannot pander to a man's intellectual arrogance, but we must cater to his intellectual integrity." The whole person, including the person's intellect and emotions and will, must be converted. If we simply convert the intellect, but do not convert the will, we won't have a Christian. In chapter four we considered the inadequacy of a mere mental assent to propositions. On the other hand, an emotional assent to Christ, divorced from mind and will, would again mean an incomplete conversion. The total personality—intellect, emotions and will—must be converted.

I would be the last one to suggest that we as Christians have all the answers to the problems of the world, or even all the answers to the problems in Christianity. By no means! One Christian, the French philosopher and mathematician Pascal, pointed out that the supreme function of reason is to show people that some things are beyond reason. However, our Lord, referring to himself, said, "You will know the truth, and the truth will set you free" (John 8:32). Surely he meant that we do have some absolutes on which to base our lives and destiny.

Without these absolutes, we have very little as Christians to offer today's world.

I am disturbed by an attitude that I sometimes discover among Christians as well as non-Christians: the suggestion that the *pursuit* of truth is more important than attaining it. These people don't really want any answers because that would end their game. For them, the search is everything. Truth itself is less attractive—a fact they often rationalize as: truth is unattainable. As a result they equate almost any answer with a pat or contrived answer.

This, to me, is dangerous thinking. An answer that is valid is not necessarily pat. "Patness" is betrayed by the attitude in which an answer is given. A pat answer comes out like the recorded song that plays when you put a nickel in the slot. The answer which takes into consideration the background of the questioner and his question and which cogently addresses itself to the point is not a pat answer. We can't alter the facts to make them fit others' presuppositions, but we can present them as a challenge to their intellectual integrity. Let's not shy away from an honest declaration of the truth which we have received.

FOUR DOCTORATES ARE NOT NECESSARY

When we think about people's questions, we often allow ourselves to be overwhelmed by the mass of information which we haven't yet mastered. Before we can give effective answers, we think we'll need to get four doctorates and a reading knowledge of 5,000 books. We get breathless just thinking about this hopeless task. Then we conclude, "I can't do it. I guess this isn't my area of witnessing." However, let me assure you, after having the privilege of witnessing to hundreds of audiences of non-Christians on almost two hundred secular campuses here and abroad, I've learned that this isn't the case.

When I began traveling I was sure I'd never survive. My first evangelistic discussion some years ago was at the University of Kansas in—of all places—a scholarship hall. I thought, "Lord, why must I begin in one of these residences reserved for brainy students on scholarships? They'll tear me apart limb from limb!" Although I didn't expect to live through that night, I did, by the grace of God and his goodness; and moreover a fellow became a Christian that evening and is faithfully serving Jesus Christ today. That night I began to acquire some valuable information. I discovered some of the questions non-Christians have on their minds and as I traveled to other campuses and spoke to more students, a pattern emerged in the questions they asked me.

In any aspect of life, all of us fear the unknown. Why don't we like to do door-to-door knocking? Some of us get the shakes just thinking about it. We're afraid because we don't know what's behind the door. Why do people fear death, basically? Until we receive Jesus Christ, death is a great unknown to us. Any experience that involves the unknown is difficult. Leading my first few discussions was a major problem for me because I didn't know what to expect. But now I can predict, with a very high degree of accuracy, the questions that will be asked me in any given discussion with non-Christians. A few of the questions may depart from the pattern, but most of them will fit into one of several basic categories.

RIGHT ANSWERS TO WRONG QUESTIONS

I recently held a mock bull session with students on a Christian college campus. They wanted to set up a typical fraternity situation so we assumed that they were the fraternity men and I'd come in to speak. I talked to them a while the way I usually do in a fraternity and then let them ask me whatever they wanted to. To my surprise, they asked all kinds of questions that had never come up in years of visiting secular campuses. Many of their questions were weighted in Christian theological terms or involved issues such as differences in Christian practices.

Most non-Christians on a secular campus are biblically illiterate, and so they ask more basic questions. This comparison indicates that the mind of the average student in a Christian school and the mind of the average non-Christian student tend to run in different channels. While this difference is understandable, it creates a problem for Christians trying to relate to non-Christians. They need to know the answers to the questions non-Christians are actually asking, rather than to be boned up on a dozen things they may never be asked about. If we have the right answers to the wrong questions, we aren't much help.

At a University of Georgia campus outreach, one of the fellows on our team had read my short articles in *HIS* magazine called "What Non-Christians Ask." After the meetings, we had a report session, and he fairly glowed. "You know, it's absolutely uncanny," he said, "I've been in three fraternities so far this week, and practically every one of these questions has come up every time!" His first experience in actual face-to-face confrontation with non-Christians' questions confirmed the pattern.

So you see, there's a pattern to the questions we'll be asked. We don't have to amass mountains of information. If we think through the answers to the common, basic questions, we'll acquire confidence and be able to help those who are asking these questions.

EIGHT BASIC QUESTIONS

Here are eight of these basic questions. Sometimes they come with slight variations, but the root question can be traced to these broader questions. I'd like to suggest briefly some of the answers I've given. You can undoubtedly improve them.

1. What About the Heathen?

Non-Christians, and many Christians too, most frequently ask about the heathen. "What about people who have never heard of Jesus Christ? Will they be condemned to hell?" At the outset I think we must acknowledge that we don't have the whole story about how God will deal with these people. He hasn't told us everything. Certain things are known to God alone. In Deuteronomy 29:29 we read, "The secret things belong to the LORD our God, but the things revealed belong to us and to our children forever." On some things God has not fully revealed his plan;

this is one instance. Our concern is to grasp fully the things he has revealed in the Scripture. On these we can rely firmly and with the utmost confidence.

First, God is just. All the evidence we have indicates that we can have confidence in his character. We can trust that whatever he does with those who have never heard of Jesus Christ will be fair. All our data indicates that God's character is just.

Second, no person will be condemned for rejecting Jesus Christ of whom he has never heard; instead, he will be condemned for violating his own moral standard, however high or low it has been. The whole world—every person, whether he has heard of the Ten Commandments or not—is in sin. Romans 2 clearly tells us that every person has a standard of some kind, and in every culture, people knowingly violate the standard they have, as anthropology has confirmed. Almost two thousand years ago, Paul explained:

> All who sin apart from the law will also perish apart from the law, and all who sin under the law will be judged by the law. For it is not those who hear the law who are righteous in God's sight, but it is those who obey the law who will be declared righteous. (Indeed, when Gentiles, who do not have the law, do by nature things required by the law, they are a law for themselves, even though they do not have the law, since they show that the requirements of the law are written on their hearts, their consciences also bearing witness, and their thoughts now accusing, now even defending them.) This will take place on the day when God will judge men's secrets through Jesus Christ, as my gospel declares. (Romans 2:12-16)

Third, Scripture indicates that every person has enough information from creation to know that God exists. This is clearly stated in Romans 1:19-20:

> What may be known about God is plain to them, because God has made it plain to them. For since the creation of the world God's invisible qualities—his eternal power and divine nature—have been clearly seen, being understood from what has been made, so that men are without excuse.

Psalm 19 confirms this fact. Then from Matthew 7:7-11 and Jeremiah 29:13 we may conclude that if people respond to the light they have and seek God, God will give them a chance to hear the truth about Jesus Christ.

Fourth, there is no indication in the Bible that people can be saved apart from Jesus Christ. This is made crystal clear. Our Lord himself declared in John 14:6, "I am the way and the truth and the life. No one comes to the Father except through me." Jesus spoke with the authority of God. Because of who he is and what he has done on the cross, it is obvious that there is no other way to God. He alone has atoned for our sins. He is the only bridge across the chasm that separates the highest possible human achievement from the infinitely holy standard of God. Peter left no room for doubt in his flat assertion in Acts 4:12, "Salvation is found in no one else, for there is no other name under heaven given to men by which we must be saved." This places tremendous responsibility on us who call ourselves Christians; we must see to it that those who have not heard do hear the gospel.

The final thing to point out to people who have raised this question is the Bible's absolute clarity concerning the judgment which awaits those who have heard the gospel, as these people have. When they face God, the issue will not be the heathen. They will have to account for what they personally have done with Jesus Christ. Sometimes people will raise the question of the heathen as a smoke screen so they can evade their personal responsibility. We need to answer this question for them, as well as think it through for our own conviction and confidence. But then, as we end the discussion, we want to swing the conversation to these people themselves and their responsibility: What are they going to do with Jesus Christ?

For a fuller discussion of the moral law inherent in the universe, see *The Case for Christianity* by C. S. Lewis.

2. Is Christ the Only Way to God?

The second question, which is a corollary or slight variation of the first, is this: "Doesn't the sincere Muslim or Buddhist or Hindu worship the same God as the Christian, but under a different name?" In other words, "Is Jesus Christ really the only way to God?"

Neither sincerity nor intensity of faith can create truth. Faith is no more valid than the object in which it is placed. Believing doesn't make something true per se, and refusing to believe a truth cannot make it false. The real issue is the question of truth.

Let's compare Islam and Christianity as an example. In the moral and ethical realms we can find many similarities between them, but the two faiths are diametrically opposed on the most crucial question: Who is Jesus Christ? Islam denies that Jesus Christ is God the Son. It denies that he died on the cross and rose from the dead. Christianity, on the other hand, affirms and focuses upon the fact that Jesus Christ, the Son of God, died on the cross for our sin and then rose from the dead. Both faiths cannot simultaneously be true at this particular point. Only one can be correct. If the crux of Christianity is false, our faith is worthless.

This question about other religions has some emotional aspects which we need to try to overcome when we discuss it. We want people to realize that Christians are not being bigoted and prejudiced or presumptuous when they say that Christ is the only way to God. As Christians we have no other option because Jesus Christ himself has said this. Although people may choose to believe whatever they wish, they have no right to redefine Christianity in their own terms. If we're going to be faithful to Jesus Christ we must stand firmly on what he said. Quite obviously, if he is God this is the only answer.

Acknowledging this, no one should feel that if we were only less bigoted our "fraternity" could get together and change its membership rules. That suggestion misses the point altogether. We're dealing with truth that has come to us by revelation, through the invasion into human history of God himself in Jesus Christ.

An illustration has often helped to make this point clear. In some areas of life, the penalties for breaking laws are socially determined. For instance, there's a stop sign on the corner. By vote the community can decide on a five-dollar, ten-dollar or fifty-dollar fine for going through that sign. Or it can abolish the fine. The penalty is not determined by the act of going through the stop sign; the legal penalty is not inherent in the violation.

But in some other aspects of life, such as in the physical realm, we find laws that are not socially determined. Suppose our community passed a unanimous resolution to suspend the law of gravity an hour a day, from 8:00 to 9:00 a.m. Who would join me in jumping off the roof to try it out? Suppose we passed the resolution three times? I still wouldn't get any takers. We do not determine socially the penalty for violating the law of gravity; the penalty is inherent in the violation. Even if we passed motions till the cows came home, the fact would remain that if you jumped off the roof someone would have to pick you up with a shovel!

In the moral realm, as in the physical, there are laws that are not socially determined. We discern these laws from what God has revealed about the inherent law of the universe. (Dorothy L. Sayers offers some further helpful thoughts on this subject in *The Mind of the Maker*.)[1]

In helping a non-Christian think through the claims to Jesus Christ to be the one way to God, our best defense is often a good offense. We don't have to be answering questions all the time. We can pose a few questions for him, too. Since he doesn't believe Christ's claim, he has some questions to answer. We can begin by asking, "Since you don't believe Jesus Christ was the Truth, which of the other three possibilities about Jesus Christ do you believe? There are only four possible conclusions about Jesus Christ and his claims. He was either a liar, a lunatic, a legend or the Truth. The person who doesn't believe he was the Truth must label him as a liar, a lunatic or a legend." Most non-Christians don't realize these are their logical options. So we've got to remind them that by saying they don't believe, they have left themselves only three alternatives.

"Which conclusion do you believe, and what evidence can you present to support this conclusion? Was he a liar?" Even those who deny his deity will invariably hasten to assure us that Jesus was a great moral philosopher and teacher. To call this good teacher a liar would be a contradiction of terms. It certainly seems improbable that he would lie about the most crucial point in his teaching, his deity.

Perhaps he was a lunatic. This conclusion would not destroy his moral integrity: He thought he was doing right, but he suffered from delusions of grandeur. We have people like this today who imagine they are Napoleon, or even Jesus Christ. The hitch in this conclusion is that the clinical symptoms of paranoia as we know it today don't jibe with the personality characteristics of Jesus Christ. In his life we find no trace of the imbalance that characterizes such people. Consider the time of his death, for instance, when he was under tremendous pressure. The poise and composure we see in him are not characteristic of people who suffer from paranoid disturbances. The biblical record gives no evidence that he was suffering from paranoia or any other mental disorder.

A third alternative is that our records about Jesus Christ are legendary. He never made some of the statements attributed to him. They were put into his mouth by overenthusiastic followers in the third or fourth century. He'd turn over in his grave if he knew the claims that have been written about him.

Modern archaeology, however, makes it increasingly difficult to maintain this theory. For instance, recent findings confirm the belief that the New Testament documents were written during the lifetime of contemporaries of Jesus Christ. The development of an elaborate legend would have required a more significant time lag. People in that skeptical age would have been no more likely to circulate and accept a legend such as this than our neighbors today would be likely to spread a report that the late President Franklin D. Roosevelt claimed to be God, said he had the power to forgive sins and rose from the dead. Too many people who knew President Roosevelt are still around. With so many testimonies to the contrary, the rumor could never get off the ground.

From here, if the person is interested, we can turn to Jesus Christ's statements about himself, using his statements in John 14. He said he was the truth, he was the way to God and anyone who sees him, sees God the Father. Any person who is intellectually honest must come to grips with these extraordinary claims.

3. Why Do the Innocent Suffer?

The third frequently asked question concerns the problem of evil. "If God is all-good and all-powerful, why do the innocent suffer? Why are some babies born blind or mentally defective or deformed? Why are wars allowed? Why . . . ?" Either God is all good, but he is not powerful enough to eliminate disease and disaster; or he is all powerful, but he is not all good and therefore he does not end all evil.

We don't have the full explanation of the origin and problem of evil because God has chosen to reveal only a part of it to us. Truly compassionate persons will find any partial explanation inadequate when faced with the horrors of evil in history and the present time.

However, there are certain things that we *do* know. We are clearly told that when God created the universe, it was perfect. Adam and Eve were given the freedom to obey God or disobey. Evil came into the universe through the first couple's disobedience. One of the inherent patterns of the universe is that our actions do not only affect us but always involve other people. Because people disobeyed and broke God's law, evil broadly pervades the universe.

As we discuss this question, it's important not to overlook the presence of evil in every one of us. Many people ask, "Why doesn't God step in and get rid of evil? Why doesn't he stomp out war?" They do not realize that if God executed judgment uniformly, not one of us would survive. Suppose God were to decree, "At midnight tonight all evil will be stamped out of the universe." Which of us would be here at 1:00 a.m.?

After we point out humankind's personal problem with evil, we need to note that God has dealt with the problem at his own expense. He not only entered human history in the Lord Jesus Christ, but he gave his life to solve the problem of evil. Every individual who willingly responds receives his gift of love, grace and forgiveness in Jesus Christ. As C. S. Lewis has observed, it is idle for us to speculate about the origin of evil. The problem we all face is the fact of evil. The only solution to the fact of evil is God's solution, Jesus Christ.

A statement made by the philosopher and theologian Francis Schaeffer in the last year of his life gives the right perspective on suffering from the Christian point of view. Dr. Schaeffer had served God very sacrificially for years and then was stricken with terminal leukemia. When asked how he reconciled the goodness of God and his present situation of imminent death, he answered, "Why shouldn't I get cancer? I live in a fallen world and am subject to all the plagues that come with that world just as the non-Christian. The difference is that I know my eternal future because I belong to Jesus Christ."

4. How Can Miracles Be Possible?
Question number four asks about miracles and opposes naturalism to supernaturalism. "How can miracles be possible? In

this scientific age, how can any intelligent person who considers the orderliness of the universe believe in them?" If we don't get to the root of this question, we may waste long hours discussing whether Christ could possibly have walked on the water, whether in fact he did feed the five thousand with five loaves and two fish, whether the children of Israel actually went through the Red Sea, and on and on. We can only answer this question if we dig down to its basic presupposition.

The real issue is whether or not God exists. If God exists, then miracles are logical and pose no intellectual contradictions. A friend of mine who grew up in Asia once told me he just couldn't quite believe that a man could become God. I saw his problem in a flash and said, "I'd have quite a time believing that, too. But I can very easily believe that God became man." There's all the difference in the world between these two concepts. By definition God is all-powerful. He can and does intervene in the universe that he has created.

Fundamentally, we're being asked, "How do I know God exists?" Without going into elaborate detail, let me give two basic thoughts. The first is the argument from design. If my computer, relatively uncomplicated as it is, doesn't exist "by chance," it seems illogical and naive to hold the position that the universe in its infinite intricacy and complexity could have developed just "by chance." Even if the individual parts were to evolve, the arrangement of those parts as a functioning whole without a designer would defy plausibility.

A second argument is based on the law of cause and effect. Could we as complex human beings be the result of a vague, ill-defined force? Given the fact that we have intellect, emotion and will, we assume that a cause greater than ourselves, having these

characteristics, brought us into being. There are innumerable illustrations we could give to develop this further.

However, the greatest indication of the existence of God is
his invading human history as a God-man. As J. B. Phillips put
it, we are "the visited planet." In answering any one of these
questions, we must eventually come to the same solution: Jesus
Christ himself. I know God exists, not because of all the philosophical arguments pro and con, but because he came into human history in Jesus Christ, and I have met him personally in
my own life. Our answer begins with him.

Because Jesus Christ claims to be God, we should examine his
claim to be truth as given in question two. From there we should
ask ourselves whether his credentials substantiate his claim and
whether he really did rise from the dead. Anyone, after all, can
make the claim to be God. I can; you can. Where I grew up in
Philadelphia there was a man who claimed to be God and called
himself "Father Divine." But with what credentials does anyone
substantiate his claim to be God? I dare say I could disprove your
claim in five minutes, and you could probably disprove mine in
two. And it's not hard to disprove the claim of the man in Philadelphia. But when we consider Jesus Christ, it's not so simple.
His credentials substantiate his claim. The supreme credential, of
course, is the fact that he rose from the dead.

Again, the question of miracles revolves around whether
there exists an all-powerful God who created the universe. If so,
we shall have little difficulty with miracles in which he transcends the natural law of which he is the author. David Hume
and others have defined a miracle as a "violation of natural law."
To take such a position, however, is to deify natural law, to cap-
italize it in such a way that whatever God there may be becomes

the prisoner of natural law, and, in effect, ceases to be God.

Christians believe in natural law; that is to say, things behave in a certain cause-and-effect way almost all the time, year after year, century after century. But in maintaining this, don't restrict God's right and power to intervene when and how he chooses. God is over, above and outside natural law and is not bound by it.

Miracles, then, are possible if we understand that they are not in conflict with any natural law. Rather, as J. N. Hawthorne puts it, "Miracles are unusual events caused by God. The laws of nature are generalizations about ordinary events caused by him."[2]

There are two views among thinking Christians as to the relationship of miracles to natural law. First, some suggest that miracles employ a "higher" natural law, which at present is unknown to us. It is quite obvious that despite all of the impressive discoveries of modern science, we are still standing on the seashore of an ocean of ignorance. If we had all the knowledge possessed by God, we would see that miracles are merely God exercising those super laws, still unknown to us. They would be the working out of the higher laws of the universe, of which we are not aware.

But a law, in the modern scientific sense, is that which is regular and acts uniformly. To say that a miracle is the result of a higher law, then, is to use the term in a way that is different from its customary usage and meaning.

The second view of miracles is the one I feel is a more appropriate view. It states that miracles are an act of creation, a sovereign, transcendent act of God's supernatural power. The biblical miracles bear scrutiny, for their list defies merely classifying under "natural" or even psychosomatic origin. Jesus raising Lazarus from the dead and the resurrection of Jesus Christ involved forces unknown to us and outside the realm of so-called natural law. The same is true of Jesus' healings. The lepers who were made well had to experience the direct power of God; the healing of the man born blind could not be accounted for on a psychosomatic basis.

In the case of the man born blind, the people observed that since the beginning of time it had not been known for a man born blind to receive his sight. And we have no more natural explanation of this miracle now than was available then. And who today has any more explanation, in a natural sense, of the resurrection of Jesus Christ from the dead than was available when it happened? No one! We simply cannot get away from the supernatural dimension of his life.

When we discuss the natural versus the supernatural, we need to point out to people what it means to prove or not prove God. Without realizing it, people probably expect proof according to the scientific method. We can never prove God by the scientific method. But this doesn't mean that our case is lost. The scientific method as a means of verification is limited to measurable aspects of reality. The scientific method, therefore, is incapable of verifying many aspects of life. No one has ever seen three feet of love or two pounds of justice, but we do not deny their reality. To insist that everything must be subjected to the scientific method for verification would be as ludicrous as to insist on measuring chlorine gas with a microphone. That's not the purpose of the microphone; we can't make it do what it has no capacity to do and deny the reality of gas in the process!

Another limitation of the scientific method is the need to verify a fact through repetition; such repetition is part of the scientific method. Now history happens to be nonrepeatable.

Since no one is ever going to repeat Napoleon, we can emphatically say that we can't prove Napoleon—by the scientific method, that is. But what does that prove? Nothing much. Because we can't repeat history, it's outside the scope of the scientific method of verification. However, there is a science of history. As we examine the data for Christianity, and particularly the evidence for the resurrection, we find a solid case on which to base our conviction.

These are the ideas we need to suggest to people who take the essentially materialistic position based on rationalistic presuppositions and claims that because there is no supernatural, miracles are impossible. When they begin with this presupposition, no amount of evidence will convince them of the truth. If you started out by denying that miracles are possible, what evidence would convince you that a miracle had taken place? None. People who say, "If God would appear to me, then I'd believe in him," are very naive. Regardless of what happened, they could explain it away in nonmiraculous, naturalistic terms if they wanted to.

Christ dealt with this problem in Luke 16:28-31, where the rich man in hell asked Abraham to send Lazarus to warn his brothers. Abraham reminded him, "They have Moses and the Prophets; let them listen to them." But the rich man said, "No, father Abraham, but if someone from the dead goes to them, they will repent." Abraham told him, "If they do not listen to Moses and the Prophets, they will not be convinced even if someone rises from the dead." The principle still holds today. The data we have concerning God's visitation to this planet are sufficient grounds for us to believe. When people refuse to accept this evidence, no additional evidence will convince them.

5. Isn't the Bible Full of Errors?

The fifth question starts out, "How do you reconcile your faith with the fact that the Bible is so full of errors?" The reliability of Scripture is being challenged. At the outset we need to ask what particular errors the person has in mind. Ninety-nine percent of the time people can't think of any. They've heard someone else say that the Bible is full of contradictions, and they've swallowed the assumption. But sometimes a person has a specific problem in mind. If you don't have the answer to his particular question, don't panic. Instead smile casually and tell him, "I don't have the answer to that one, but I'll be glad to dig it up for you." Volumes have been written on some of these topics. After two thousand years, no one this week is going to think of the question that will bring Christianity crashing down.

If people haven't read the Bible, that's a fair indication of their insincerity in questioning it. But don't press this point with them. Under no circumstances should we make fun of anyone or try to argue by ridicule. This is deadly behavior when we're talking to people about these important issues. Some of the greatest damage to the Christian faith has been caused by those who, though meaning well, attempted to win their case by ridiculing the others' positions. They only brought the gospel into disrepute.

The Bible does contain some apparent contradictions. However, our friends probably don't realize that time and time again an apparent contradiction has been vindicated by the discoveries of modern archaeology. Noted contemporary archaeologist Keith N. Schoville makes this remarkable statement, "It is important to realize that archaeological excavations have produced ample evidence to prove unequivocally that the Bible is not a pious forgery. Thus far, no historical statement in the Bible has been proven false on the basis of evidence retrieved through archaeological research."[3]

For those still-unreconciled conflicts between the Bible and history, our logical attitude should be to wait and see what further evidence will disclose. We don't have all the answers to all the problems. But all the vindicating data thus far certainly suggest that we can trust the biblical record about those details that still appear questionable.

Evolution is a problem in evangelism only insofar as it leads to an atheistic conclusion. It is unwise to get involved in a technical discussion about evolution because it isn't the real issue. I usually ask, "What conclusion are you drawing from your evolutionary position—that the universe happened by chance? Or are you saying that God created the universe and did so by using certain evolutionary processes? I'm not convinced about that particular position, but let's assume for the moment it's correct. What conclusion are you drawing?" From there I direct the person's attention to what Jesus Christ has said and done. How God brought the universe into being is not so important as that he did it.

One's presupposition and not the actual evidence often determines a person's conclusion. If people are trying to suggest that God is not the author of creation and that the universe did happen by chance, then we need to discuss this problem with them. A seemingly strong case for a naturalistic position can be made by ignoring the evidence for Jesus Christ. An amazing number of thinking non-Christians have never really considered his incarnation and the implications of it on this question.

6. Isn't Christian Experience Only Psychological?

The sixth question is subtle and can become rather personal: "Isn't it possible to explain Christian experience in purely psychological terms?" Some people suggest that we have faith only because we've been conditioned since our early childhood to this way of thinking and living. They think we've been raised like Pavlov's dogs. But they oversimplify the situation. Anyone who has traveled widely and met other Christians knows that preconditioning can't explain many conversions, for Christians have been converted from every imaginable background. Thousands of them had no childhood contact with Christianity, yet all will testify that a personal encounter with Jesus Christ transformed their lives. In their studies, psychologists try to keep all but one or two factors constant. To verify their conclusions they must eliminate as many variables as possible. But in comparing the lives of Christians, Jesus Christ is the only constant factor.

From one case history to the next all other details may vary. Only Jesus remains the same. He alone makes a thief honest, a profligate pure, a liar truthful. It is he who can fill a hate-ridden heart with love.

Other psychology-minded people assert that ideas of spiritual reality are essentially wish fulfillments. All religious experience, they contend, can be traced to people feeling a need for God, creating an image in their minds and then worshiping the mental projection. His supposed spiritual reality, of course, lacks any objective reality. Again and again we hear religion called the crutch of people who can't get along in life. This view raises a valid issue which we must consider.

How can we know that we haven't hypnotized ourselves into believing what we want to believe? If our spiritual experience is just a result of wish fulfillment or positive thinking, we should be able to regard any object, a pipe organ for instance, as God. If we think about the pipe organ as God long enough, it will become God to us; then lo and behold, we've a subjective experience. But what is our objective evidence for this subjective experience?

Let's try another situation. Suppose someone wanders into your room with a fried egg dangling over his left ear and says, "Man, this fried egg is the most! I get joy, peace, satisfaction and purpose in life from it. Tremendous, man—this fried egg is really It." What do you say? In the final analysis you can't argue with experience. That's why a Christian's testimony is so effective; no one can argue with it. Neither can you argue with this fried-egg guy.

But you can investigate his experience by asking him several crucial questions (the same questions that Christians should be prepared to answer about their own experiences). How do you know it's the fried egg and not autohypnosis that's giving you this satisfaction and peace? Who else has gotten the same benefits out of the egg? To what objective fact is this experience tied? Christianity differs from autohypnosis, wish fulfillments and all the other psychological phenomena in that the Christian's subjective experience is securely bound to an objective, historical fact—namely, the resurrection from the dead of Jesus Christ.

A professor in semantics from the University of California in Berkeley recently attended a series of meetings where I was the speaker. He was a complete relativist in his thinking. Right in the middle of my talks he would stand up in the audience and interpret (and briefly refute) what I had said. I'll admit it was all done in good spirit, but it was a bit unnerving too.

He advanced the popular idea that what we believe is true to us is not necessarily true for other people, and he used this illustration: A man may be tied on a railroad track in a fraternity hazing. When the train whizzes by on the next track, he dies of a heart attack because he doesn't know that it's not on his track. As far as he's concerned the train might as well have been on the first track. He believed it was and so it became true for him. You see, what's true for you may not be true for me.

Time and time again we tried to show this professor the significant difference in Christianity, that is, the fact of the resurrection. About the fourth time around, the penny dropped. Standing at the blackboard with a piece of chalk in his hand, he suddenly stopped in the middle of a sentence and said, "Hmm . . . yes. That would make quite a difference," and sat down.

If the resurrection is true, it makes all the difference in the world. It is the confirmation of God's revelation in Christ, an absolute truth, a historical fact outside of ourselves, an objective fact to which our subjective experience is tied. We need to hold these two facts, the objective and the subjective, in proper perspective. The fact that Jesus Christ rose from the dead means nothing to me personally or experientially until I receive him as Lord and Savior in my own life. On the other hand, if I have only my own experience, I'll sooner or later begin wondering if it is real or merely self-suggestion. I need to recognize that my experience is based on the solid foundation of an objective fact in history.

A thorough grasp of the resurrection of Jesus Christ is our objective foundation. For a brief and helpful summary, read the InterVarsity Press booklet *The Evidence for the Resurrection* by J. N. D. Anderson, a professor of oriental law at London University. He discusses the evidence and the various alternatives that have been advanced to explain away the resurrection. He shows why, in the light of the data, each argument against the resurrection is inadequate.

7. Won't a Good, Moral Life Get Me to Heaven?

The seventh question reflects a very prevalent attitude of our age. "Isn't living a good moral life all I need to do to get to heaven?" Or as a student at Duke University said after a discussion, "If God grades on the curve, I'll make it." His words are an apt summary of the confusion today about religion in general. Most people will accept this philosophy that all we need to do is our best, and then everything will be all right, or at least we'll be able to squeak by. In this wistful hope we see an incredible optimism about humanity's righteousness and an appalling ignorance of God's infinite holiness. God doesn't grade on the curve. He has an absolute standard, Jesus Christ.

Light, when it is turned on, destroys darkness. Likewise, the character of God so blazes in its purity that it consumes all evil. If we came to him without any help, we could not abide in his presence but would be consumed because of the corruption in our lives. The perfect righteousness of Jesus Christ is the only basis on which we can come into fellowship with the living God.

An illustration helps people to see their misunderstanding here. Suppose the entire human race lined up on the West Coast with one objective, to get to Hawaii. We'll equate their goal with God's standard of righteousness. The gun is fired and all the swimmers jump in. As we watch the swimmers we see the most moral person of all. She's been a wonderful professor and a good person, always doing her best and following high moral standards; yet she would be the first to admit her imperfection and sinfulness. But she's out there in the water seventy-five miles from shore.

Next we pick out the Joe College Fellow who's not quite ready for Sing-Sing or Cook County Jail. He does cheat on exams a little and goes on a binge now and then; he gets into a few scrapes and does things that are wrong. But he's not really too bad. He's gotten about ten miles out. A derelict from Skid Row is practically drowning one hundred and fifty yards off-shore. Scattered about in the water between the two extremes of the spectrum we see the rest of the human race. As we look from the bum on Skid Row to the Joe College type to the tremendously moral professor who's gone seventy-five miles, we see the difference. It's an enormous difference. But what's the difference in terms of Hawaii? Everyone will drown.

A set of swimming instructions won't help at this point. We need somebody who will *take* us to Hawaii. This is where Jesus Christ comes in. If you can make it to Hawaii by yourself, if you can live a life that is absolutely perfect in thought, word and deed, you can make it to heaven on your own steam. But no man ever has or ever will succeed. All the other religions of the world are essentially sets of swimming instructions, suggested codes of ethics for a wonderful pattern of life.

But people's basic problem is not lack of knowledge about what they ought to do; it is lacking the power to live as they ought. The good news of Christianity is that Jesus Christ, who invaded human history, does for us what we couldn't possibly do for ourselves. Through him we may be reconciled to God, given his righteousness and enabled to have fellowship with him in his very presence.

8. Isn't Faith Believing Something That Isn't True?

There is one issue that may not be posed as a question, but I will often take initiative in raising it. It usually rivets the attention of the person I'm talking to. It is this: faith is commonly equated with superstition. Have you ever heard someone say that in order to have faith you must kiss your brains good-bye? "I'm too intelligent to be taken in by faith," they say.

Non-Christians aren't the only ones who feel like that, though. Some Christians also equate faith with superstition. Deep down they accept the Sunday-school youngster's definition of faith: "It's believing something that you know isn't true." A lot of us, if we're honest about it, may feel the very same way. A few simple facts about faith can even help us understand some of these answers we've discussed.

Daily Experience

First of all, faith is a common occurrence for all. It is widely mistaken as a phenomenon reserved for emotionally disturbed people who can't make it in life without a crutch. Yet these very people who view faith as a prop or tranquilizer exercise faith every day of their lives. You've probably eaten at least one meal today that you didn't prepare yourself or see being prepared. As you ate, you had no way of knowing if that food contained poison, but you ate it nonetheless—in faith. Perhaps it was blind faith; you may be suffering from food poisoning an hour from now. Probably, though, you ate the meal because you had confidence in the one who cooked it, even though it was in a restaurant and the cook was unknown to you. You exercised reasonable faith. Students also have faith in their academic institutions and expect them to grant a degree when the prescribed courses are completed.

All scientific research and progress depends on faith, too. Although the objectivity of science and scientists is often stressed, their work rests on several unproved axioms which must be accepted—if you'll pardon the expression—by faith. Scientists start by believing there is an orderly reality to be observed. They also believe that causal laws apply to that reality. That is to say, every cause has an effect. And finally, they believe that human logic is adequate to describe physical reality—even to understand the universe. These axioms are implicitly accepted and rarely ever questioned. Thus, faith is a genuine experience of every one of us. What we face is not, "Do we have faith or not?" but "In what and to what extent do we have faith?"

VALIDITY OF FAITH

Faith, I would argue, is only as valid as the object (the person or thing) in which it is placed. Maybe you have implicit faith in your brother. If he asks to borrow fifty dollars this afternoon, and you have fifty dollars, you'll give it to him. But suppose that, unknown to you, he has disgraced the family in some way and is leaving town for good. All your faith and confidence in him won't bring back your money after he disappears tomorrow, never to return. Your faith in him can be only as valid as he is trustworthy.

Or we might think of a diseased little girl whose father takes her through the jungle to the witch doctor. The father may have implicit faith in the concoction being brewed to cure her. But no matter how much he believes in the potion, his faith won't save his daughter's life if the brew is poison. Faith is no more valid than the object in which it is placed. His faith is no more than superstition.

This principle has a corollary: intense belief does not create truth. Faith's validity cannot be increased by intensity. We find a lot of naive thinking about this in the world today. People say, "Well, I think it's just wonderful that you can believe that. It's true for you, even though it's not true for me." Believing doesn't make a wish true. The generalizations in which we trust may be pure superficialities. When a little old lady was robbed by a young man who had rented one of her rooms, she sadly said, "My, but he was such a nice boy. He even had YMCA on his towels!" Although she still wanted to believe in his integrity, her belief couldn't create an objective truth. Belief does not create truth any more than failure to believe destroys truth.

Some years ago a man in Texas received word that he had inherited a large fortune from a relative in England. This Texan, a recluse living in poverty, had never heard of the English relative. Even though he was on the verge of starvation he wouldn't believe the news. His refusal to believe didn't change that fact that he was heir to a million dollars; instead, disbelief deprived him of enjoying the money. He died starving and poverty-stricken. The objective truth remained, but he missed out on its benefits because he failed to claim them in faith.

In the realm of everyday human experience, we tend to treat facts as facts. Few of us have trouble accepting the concept that belief can't create, and disbelief can't destroy, objective facts. But when talking about God, many people are strangely naive. I've heard more than one student say, "Oh, I don't believe in God," as though that settled the question. And a friend will say, "Heaven and hell? I can't believe that they're real places." Then he doesn't need to worry about them, he thinks; by disbelieving he has supposedly wiped them out of existence.

Dr. A. W. Tozer's distinction between *faith* and *superstition* may help us here. Faith sees the invisible but it does not see the nonexistent. As Hebrews 11:1 explains it, "Now faith is being sure of what we hope for and certain of what we do not see." The eyes of faith see something that is real, although invisible. What superstition sees is unreal and nonexistent. As we learn to discern between unreality and invisible reality, we discover a world of difference between the two.

To repeat: Everyone believes in something. The object of people's faith, not the intensity of their belief or disbelief, will determine their faith's validity. Faith placed in something unreal is only superstition.

Since the object of the Christian's faith is the Lord Jesus Christ, we must ask ourselves whether Jesus Christ is a valid object for our faith. Many people, after studying the facts, have concluded that he is. Now, by putting the hypothesis to the test of personal experience through a relationship with him, we are proving his absolute trustworthiness.

THE BASIC PROBLEM IS MORAL

Now that we've briefly thought through these questions, we need to be reminded that ultimately humankind's basic problem is not intellectual; it's moral. Once in a while our answer won't satisfy people. Their rejection of the answer doesn't invalidate it. On the other hand, they may be convinced and still not become a Christian. I've had people tell me, "You've answered every one of my questions to my satisfaction." After thanking them for the flattery I've asked, "Are you going to become a Christian then?" and they've smiled a little sheepishly, "Well, no." "Why not?" I've inquired. "Frankly, it would mean too radical a change in my way of life."

Many people are not prepared to let anyone else, including God, run their lives. It's not that they can't believe; but they won't believe. They at least see what the issue is. Our responsibility in using the information in this chapter is to help them reach this point of understanding.

People often ask, "If Christianity is true, why do the majority of intelligent people not believe it?" The answer is precisely the same as the reason the majority of unintelligent people don't believe it. They don't want to! They're unwilling to accept the moral demands it would make on their lives. We can take a horse to water, but we can't make him drink. People must be willing to believe before they ever will believe. There isn't a thing you or I can do with people who, despite all evidence to the contrary, insist that black is white.

We ourselves must be convinced about the truth we proclaim. Otherwise we won't be at all convincing to other people. We must be able to say confidently with Peter, "We did not follow cleverly invented stories when we told you about the power and coming of our Lord Jesus Christ" (2 Peter 1:16). Then our witness will ring with authority, conviction and the power of the Holy Spirit.

Questions for Individual or Group Study

1. 1 Peter 3:15 commands us to "Always be prepared to give an answer to everyone who asks you to give the reason for the hope that you have. But do this with gentleness and respect." Are you having any trouble obeying, or even wanting to obey, this command? If so, why?

2. Paul Little suggests that Christians sometimes hold two harmful attitudes when it comes to dealing with questions

concerning faith: that asking questions is wrong and that answering questions will automatically bring people to Jesus (pp. 126-27). Why would Christians feel this way?

3. What are the negative effects of such attitudes?

4. What is your reaction when someone brings up questions about Christianity? How could you handle the situation better?

5. In dealing with people's questions, it is important to understand their motivation for asking and then to seek to reassure the people if we can. Listed here are the eight questions the author has found non-Christians often ask:

- What about the heathen?
- Is Christ the only way to God?
- Why do the innocent suffer?
- How can miracles be possible?
- Isn't the Bible full of errors?
- Isn't Christian experience only psychological?
- Won't a good, moral life get me to heaven?
- Isn't faith believing something that isn't true?

For two or more of the questions, determine what admirable quality is motivating the person to ask this question.

6. If asked those questions, what would you seek to reassure the person of?

7. After reading the chapter, do you think you have a ready answer to these basic questions? If not, what further preparation will you do?

8. The author says, "I recently held a mock bull session with students on a Christian college campus. . . . They asked all

kinds of questions that had never come up in years of visiting secular campuses" (p. 130). As people's knowledge of Christianity grows, so too can the range and depth of their questions. If you are one of these people or know others who are, how can you work to get these questions answered?

9. Write out your own reasons for believing Christ is the only way to God.

SUGGESTIONS FOR A STUDY-GROUP LEADER

1. Allow group members to share how they applied last week's study. You may want to discuss why they succeeded or failed to carry out their personal applications.

2. If group members wrote out their rationales for believing Christ is the only way to God, have members critique one another's papers, mentioning the paper's strong points (clear, practical, logical) and weak points (illogical, inconsistent or unscriptural). Discuss critiques as a group in a positive way.

7

Christ Is Relevant Today

—————— 🌿 ——————

The question uppermost in the minds of people today is not, Is Christianity true? They have a more practical question on their minds: Is it relevant? Student reaction is often: "So I believe what you've said about Jesus Christ—so what? What's it got to do with modern life? What's it got to do with me?" If we want to speak of Jesus Christ today, we need to have in the forefront of our minds how he is personally relevant to us. From there we can consider how to relate the events that took place two thousand years ago to life in the twentieth century.

This is a day when conversations about spiritual realities are part of everyday social interchange. The day of the taboo on "religion and politics" is gone. And the need for such discussion couldn't be greater. Shortly before his death, the late Dr. Karl Compton of Massachusetts Institute of Technology warned that humankind faces annihilation unless the human race soon achieves moral and spiritual advances equivalent to its technological advances.

Life magazine, in reporting the Nobel prize winners in physics several years ago, pointed out that the tremendously rapid advances in scientific understanding have been mere arithmetic gains in comparison to the geometric gains of ignorance. Each additional discovery multiplies our realization of how much we do not know and cannot control. It also enables us to manipulate extensive new areas for ill as well as for good. For instance, nuclear energy can be used to destroy cities or cancer. Genetic engineering that is designed to aid us can backfire into unthinkable disasters. In spite of the fact that many attempt to keep morality separate from science, ethical and metaphysical issues are more openly investigated and to the point today than ever before.

Inner Emptiness

Many thoughtful people now realize that they cannot subsist on a diet of platitudes. How is the living Christ relevant to them? In considering present and eternal human needs, we find that the relevance of Jesus Christ to twentieth-century people is disclosed by his own words. The "I am" designations recorded in the Gospel of John give us a clue as we see their relationship to modern people and their needs.

One basic need is for a filling of the spiritual vacuum, an answer to the inner emptiness that plagues many lives today. People often immerse themselves, in fact, lose themselves, in all kinds of activity and external stimulation. Remove that external stimulation, get them alone with their thoughts, and they're bored, anxious or miserable. They feel the aching void within, and they can't escape it. They realize their lack of inner resources for the tests of life; all their props are external. Nothing external can produce lasting satisfaction. Satisfaction that lasts must come from what is inside us.

The Lord Jesus Christ says in John 6:35, "I am the bread of life. He who comes to me will never go hungry, and he who believes in me will never be thirsty."

A tremendous thing happens when we become personally related to Jesus Christ as a living person. He enters our inner beings and fills our spiritual vacuums as only he can. Because he is inside us through the indwelling presence of the Holy Spirit, we can have ultimate satisfaction. Augustine and many others throughout the centuries have echoed this discovery: "Thou hast made us for Thyself, O God, and our hearts are restless till they find their rest in Thee." God constructed us this way— creatures dependent on our Creator for completion and fulfillment. We can function as our Maker intended only when he is occupying the very center of our lives.

Being released from dependence on external things for stimulation and pleasure in life is like sitting down to a sirloin steak after months of eating potato peelings. When we stop depending on outward and material things, we don't have to stop enjoying them. We can enjoy a concert, for instance, or the beauty of a sunset, to the glory of God. But we no longer depend on these things for our satisfaction in life. Like our Lord, we have food to eat which others do not, namely, doing the will of our Father in heaven (John 4:32). We draw from the resources that we have within us through the Lord Jesus Christ. We enjoy but do not depend on externals.

Jesus Christ is "the thing" many people are longing to get hold of. He is the one who will fill their aching void and free them from their false dependencies.

Purposelessness

Another major area of need is the aimlessness, the purposelessness that characterizes our age. I see it repeatedly in the student world. Many come up to me after a discussion and say, "You described me exactly. I don't know what I'm doing here in the university. I don't know why I'm eating three meals a day, studying architecture (physics, or whatever). I'm here because my folks are paying the bill, but I can't see what it's all about or what it's all leading to. I'm caught in a rat race of daily routines. It's hard to keep plugging away at the books when you can't see where you're going or why."

To this need the Lord Jesus Christ says, "I am the light of the world. Whoever follows me will never walk in darkness, but will have the light of life" (John 8:12).

When we follow the Lord we discover a purpose and direction for our lives, because we are living in the light of God himself and of his will for us. We are no longer fumbling in the darkness of confusion. Have you ever groped about in a dark room trying to find the light switch? You brush against something. Then you feel something else trail across your face. You jump three feet and knock over a waste basket. Your heart skips a beat. You know this uncertain, insecure feeling. At last you find the light switch, turn it on and orient yourself. Immediately you're secure. You know exactly how to proceed. Our experience is similar when we come to know the Lord Jesus Christ. He leads us out of our confusion and uncertainty into his light. We see our lives in the context of God's will and purpose for history. That vision bestows significance, meaning and purpose.

Most of God's will is already revealed for us in Scripture. When we are obeying the will of God as we know it, he will make more of the details of his will clear to us. When we have told him we're ready to accept his will whatever it may be, he gradually discloses to us additional details about where we should be and what we should do. As a scroll unwinds, so he shows to us, his children, his divine purposes.

These details, which mean so much to us individually, are in one sense quite incidental to the basic purpose of God. He is calling out for himself a people from every tribe and tongue and nation, a people who will individually manifest the likeness of Christ. This is what God is doing in history. When he brings history to its conclusion, you and I will have the privilege of being part of God's eternal work.

Our lives have significance, meaning and purpose not only for this life but for eternity. Think of it! Many people have some purpose in life at this moment. But most of these purposes are short-lived. They won't give ultimate satisfaction; they don't mean a thing in terms of eternity. To have ultimate meaning our lives must count not only for time, but also for eternity. We see so many people today who don't know what life is all about; they're groping around in darkness without Christ. They're as aimless as a ship without a rudder. If we relate the Lord Jesus Christ to them as the one who fulfills our need for direction and makes life purposeful, they may be attracted to him and let him meet their needs.

FEAR OF DEATH

A third need that the Lord Jesus Christ can meet is our need for an antidote to the fear of death. When we're young, death tends to be academic. We don't expect to die soon, so we don't give the possibility much thought. But death can rapidly become a prime consideration.

In this nuclear age, an amazing number of young people have begun to think hard about death. They're keenly aware that we live on the brink of destruction. One push of a button and everything could be gone. In a 1984 national opinion poll, George Gallup asked which problem facing the United States was felt to be the most serious. The overwhelming majority of those polled listed the threat of annihilation by nuclear war as our primary threat in this decade as well as in the year 2000.[1] While not always in the forefront of our thinking, the destructiveness of the bomb lurks beneath the surface. It is not only that we possess the power to destroy civilization but any one of our enemies in the "nuclear club" also has that capability.

Frantically we try to avoid other forms of imminent death by lessening alcohol consumption, avoiding cholesterol and not smoking. The *New York Times* reported that with these restrictions a forty-five-year-old man can live about eleven years longer, a forty-five-year-old woman could add an extra seven years to her life.[2] Then around the corner comes the as-yet-uncontrollable killer AIDS. Young people fear contamination by person-to-person contact. Older people fear infection through illnesses that require blood transfusions. The slow-moving train of death cannot be avoided, nor can it be faced.

To this kind of fearful world the Lord Jesus Christ speaks with power about death. In John 11:25-26, he says, "I am the resurrection and the life. He who believes in me will live, even though he dies; and whoever lives and believes in me will never die." As we come to know him in personal experience, Jesus Christ delivers us from the fear of death. Death ceases to be an unknown. We know it is simply the servant that ushers us into the presence of the living God whom we love. This knowledge enabled Paul to exult, "Where, O death, is your victory? Where, O death, is your sting?" (1 Corinthians 15:55). Instead of fearing death, we anticipate the most dynamic experience we can ever have.

I hope none of us has succumbed to the naive impression that heavenly existence is sitting on Pink Cloud Number Nineteen and strumming a harp. Naturally, we'd all be terribly bored with heaven after the first week. Lest we fall for such silly thoughts, let's be assured that heaven will not be a boring place. We don't have all the details, because God hasn't chosen to give them to us; but from what he has told us we can conclude that heaven will be a dynamic, expanding, creative experience far beyond anything our finite minds can now comprehend. It will be the essence of joy and satisfaction and song. Even though we don't fully understand what heaven will be, we look forward to being forever with the Lord. So we can suggest to others that Jesus Christ himself is the solution to their present fears of death.

Until we ourselves face the prospect of death, however, we may not be sure experientially that Christ delivers us from this fear. It's wonderfully easy to say he does, as you relax with friends around a warm fire after a scrumptious meal. It's quite different to say it when you're actually facing death.

Situations such as impending surgery often bring individuals face to face with the fact of dying. When I underwent heart surgery at age twenty-four, I saw in the depths of my own experience Christ's power to conquer the fear of dying. This proof was a valuable byproduct of the operation. Before, I'd always maintained that Christians don't fear death, but I couldn't speak from personal experience.

When they came in to inject the anesthetic the morning of the operation, I was keenly aware of my chances. This was before the days of life-support systems, and my surgeon had never done this particular procedure on an adult. I knew that in all likelihood I would come back from the operating room, and yet there was that other chance! A heart operation, you know, can be a complete success, but the patient may die because one of seventy-four other things has gone wrong.

Well, that morning as I was wheeled toward the operating room, a joy and peace that had to come from outside of myself flooded my being. I'll never forget it. If I'd ever thought that peace in the face of death could be conjured up through the power of positive thinking, that idea was dispelled forever. I knew I didn't have it in me to face this crisis myself. Mortal fear had gripped the man across the hall who was going in for an appendectomy. If positive thinking could have done the trick, he could have talked himself out of his fear.

As for me, strains of *Messiah* pounded through my brain as I was rolled down the hall to the operating room. As the nurses dripped in the sodium pentothal, I could even joke with them about how long I would stay awake—I think I got to six before I lost consciousness. It was a wonderful experience for me to put this fact of reality to the test and prove it true. Because it is true, we can invite those seeking freedom from the fear of death to turn to the Lord Jesus Christ and find him a relevant solution to their fear.

Desire for Inner Peace

Another expression of need today is the longing for inner peace. A Christian doctor on the West Coast took an informal, three-year poll among his patients. He wanted to know what one wish each would make if assured that the wish would be granted. Peace of heart, mind and soul was the number one desire of 87 percent of his patients. The phenomenal sale of religious books in recent years also indicates this unmet need. People don't have inner peace, but they want it desperately. Deep down they realize that everything in this life—material possessions, power, prestige, fame—will turn to dust and ashes. They yearn for the lasting inner peace and contentment that transcends these passing things.

Again, our Lord Jesus himself supplies the answer to humanity's need. His promise in John 14:27 is more than sufficient: "Peace I leave with you; my peace I give you. I do not give to you as the world gives. Do not let your hearts be troubled."

His peace differs from the peace the world gives. The peace we find in the world may seem very real for the moment, but then it's gone. Jesus said he was not of the world (John 17:14). Therefore he can give a peace that transcends this world, a peace that is deep-seated, permanent, eternal. This deep-seated peace of heart, mind and soul grows out of our personal relationship of faith and dependence on the Lord Jesus Christ. He only asks us to accept his invitation, "Come to me, all you who are weary and burdened, and I will give you rest" (Matthew 11:28). People would pay millions of dollars if rest could be bought with money. But it's not available that way. The Lord Jesus Christ only gives his peace to those who will receive it as a free gift.

LONELINESS

Although we all have a basic need for love and security, loneliness is common today. A Harvard sociologist, David Riesman, emphasized this fact in his much-read book *The Lonely Crowd*.[3] He points out that many people are only existing as shells in the midst of a crowd.

Our Lord has dynamically related himself to this particular need in saying, "I am the good shepherd. The good shepherd lays down his life for the sheep" (John 10:11).

A shepherd looks after and cares for the sheep. Our Lord cared so much that he gave his life for his sheep. He has further assured us with the words, "I am with you always, to the very end of the age" and "I will never leave you nor forsake you."

A student from Barnard College of Columbia University came to see my wife one afternoon while we were living in New York City. The woman was utterly alone and felt she couldn't trust anyone because of past experiences with family and friends. As Marie told her about some of the ways Jesus Christ would meet the needs in her life, she looked up with tears in her eyes and asked, "Do you mean that he would never leave me; that he would always love me if I committed my life to him?" My wife assured her that she meant just that, for the authority of our Lord's words and the proof of her own personal experience confirmed his faithfulness.

Has the presence of Jesus Christ ever dispelled your loneliness? Because I do a lot of traveling, I often find myself alone in Boondocks Junction, not knowing anyone. It's been wonderful at such times to claim the reality of the Lord's presence by faith and to recognize that I am never alone. It's tremendous knowing that we will never be alone because the Lord Jesus Christ is always with us. Sometimes when we imagine we're all alone, we're tempted to do things that we wouldn't do if we remembered Christ's abiding presence with us. But when we consciously recognize and live in the light of his presence, we have a negative deterrent from sin as well as a positive dynamic for life.

LACK OF SELF-CONTROL

Many people face a problem of poor self-control: "I find myself doing things I never thought I'd indulge in. I vow I'm going to change, but I can't." When students open up about themselves, they almost always admit this problem. They've become involved in campus behavior that they would never have dreamed of back home. The maelstrom of social pressure sucks them in. Then, try as they will, they can't escape its grasp.

Our Lord speaks to this need by promising to give us life and power. In John 14:6 he says, "I am the way and the truth and the life."

As we rely on him, avoiding the temptations we would bring upon ourselves and trusting in his power to deliver us from the temptations that come unforeseen, he releases his power in our lives and transforms our lack of self-control into deliverance from the power of sin. This transforming power characterizes the lives of many who have come to know Jesus Christ. It is especially evident in people who have been converted out of pagan backgrounds into a drastically different pattern of life. Jesus Christ has broken their chains of lack of self-control and given them power that they know couldn't come from themselves. This is one of the most potent relevancies of Jesus Christ to twentieth-century humanity.

OUR THINKING NEEDS INTEGRATION

In his words "I am the way and the truth and the life," our Lord also speaks to another major need we have: integration in our thinking.

A University of Wisconsin senior approached a Christian faculty friend of mine with this problem: "I've completed my 144 credit hours, and in two weeks I'm going to graduate. But I feel like I'm leaving the university with a bagful of marbles in my hand. I don't see any relationships between the various courses I've studied. They don't seem to fit together. They're more like unrelated marbles in a bag." This fellow did not know him who is the Truth—the one who is absolute truth, from whom all truth stems, in whom all truth is interrelated and tied together. All kinds of things begin to fall into place in Jesus Christ as we come to see him as the one who ultimately is the only truth.

We have authority as Christians to speak of Jesus Christ because he is the Truth. We shouldn't communicate the gospel on mere pragmatic grounds, although the gospel is true pragmatically. Our approach does not present God as a cosmic bellboy who meets all our needs. We don't claim that Christianity is true because it works. No, Christianity works because it is true. Jesus Christ is the Truth.

Our Lord spoke with devastating authority when he said, "Heaven and earth will pass away, but my words will never pass away" (Mark 13:31). The message of Jesus Christ has a down-to-earth, pragmatic effect for one who trusts him. Though this is true, this is only one aspect of the message; it is not the message itself. Our primary message should be the revealed truth of God concerning our need for repentance and the redemption available through Jesus Christ. Then we can relate Jesus Christ to contemporary needs, showing the people around us that he can be relevant to them in personal experience. Our own personal experience of how Jesus Christ meets specific needs will help others to see how very relevant and reliable the promises of Jesus Christ are.

In this short chapter we certainly haven't covered all the

needs of people in today's world, nor all the Lord's specific provisions for each of them. Neither are we pretending that once we receive Jesus Christ all our struggles are over. The Christian life is a warfare, and the two combatants, Jesus Christ and Satan, never call a draw. The profound, unchanging truth is that our Lord is the victor and is with us in the battle, and he makes all the difference in the world.

QUESTIONS FOR INDIVIDUAL OR GROUP STUDY

1. How can we be diligent in defending truth and still be irrelevant to our hearers?

2. "We don't claim that Christianity is true because it works. No, Christianity works because it is true. Jesus Christ is the Truth" (p. 170). How much should our presentation of the good news be oriented toward the needs it will meet rather than the fact that it is true?

3. Inner emptiness, purposelessness, fear of death, inner turmoil, loneliness, lack of self-control. Paul Little shows from personal experience how Christ can make a big difference in these areas. Do you think it is possible for people not to realize they have needs—and therefore not know they need Christ's help?

4. How can we approach people who seem more "together" than we are ourselves?

5. Can a person who is not a Christian have any of these needs met without Christ? Why or why not?

6. How should this affect our presentation of the gospel to that person?

7. When we share with others about Christ's ability to meet

needs, we can't fall back on Little's experience alone. What circumstances in your own life show that knowing Christ has made a difference?

8. Who in particular might benefit from hearing your experiences? How could you accomplish this?

Suggestions for a Study-Group Leader

1. Allow group members to share how they applied last week's study. You may want to discuss why they succeeded or failed to carry out their personal applications.

2. If some members of your group can remember, ask them to identify the biggest needs they had in their own lives before accepting Christ as Savior and Lord. Were those needs what led them to faith in God, directly or indirectly? Has Jesus met those needs?

8

Worldliness
External or Internal?

Genuine Christians want to live holy lives. James urged that we keep ourselves unpolluted by the world (James 1:27). Paul repeated the Old Testament command, "Come out from them and be separate, says the Lord. Touch no unclean thing" (2 Corinthians 6:17, quoting Isaiah 52:11). Peter voiced God's requirement more positively, "Be holy, because I am holy" (1 Peter 1:16). Today even well-meaning friends and pastors are apt to exhort us with these and similar verses but without explaining them sensibly.

SEPARATION IS NOT ISOLATION

Much of our fuzzy thinking about holiness stems from falsely equating separation with isolation. A medical analogy may help us. When the Center for Disease Control fears an epidemic of scarlet fever, it tries to isolate the germ carriers. If everyone who has the disease is quarantined, the disease won't spread. Similarly, a sure preventive against the spread of the gospel is to isolate its carriers (Christians) from everyone else. This can't be what Christ would have for us!

It is Satan who tries to convince us that if we clan together and avoid all unnecessary contact with non-Christians, we will not be contaminated by the world around us. By his devilish logic he has persuaded us that true spirituality is to separate ourselves totally from the world around us. Some Christians have told me with evident pride that no non-Christian has ever been inside their homes. With an air of "spirituality," they have boasted that they have no non-Christian friends. No wonder they have never had the joy of introducing someone to the Savior!

When we reexamine the New Testament's teaching, we discover that separation from the world involves pulling back from and avoiding the evil, as in "touch nothing unclean." But in view of other teachings, it cannot be teaching isolation from the world! In his prayer for us in John 17, the Lord Jesus made this clear: "My prayer is not that you take them out of the world but that you protect them from the evil one" (v. 15). And having safely entrusted us to the Father for our protection, he left his followers with this command: "Therefore go and make disciples of all nations . . ." for "you will be my witnesses . . . to the ends of the earth" (Matthew 28:19; Acts 1:8).

Our present confusion between *isolation* and *separation* is no new problem, though. We detect the same misunderstanding among the first-century Corinthians to whom Paul explained,

> I have written you in my letter not to associate with sexually immoral people—not at all meaning the people of

this world who are immoral, or the greedy and swindlers, or idolaters. In that case you would have to leave this world. But now I am writing you that you must not associate with anyone who calls himself a brother but is sexually immoral or greedy, an idolater or a slanderer, a drunkard or a swindler. With such a man do not even eat. (1 Corinthians 5:9-11)

The Christians in Corinth needed to realize, as we do, that withdrawal from those who do not know Jesus Christ is outright disobedience to the will of the Lord.

In the light of this, what do we mean by *spiritual* and by *worldly?* How we view these terms deeply affects our own everyday lives as well as the impression we give to young Christians, especially those converted from non-Christian backgrounds. In fact, it colors the advice we give others about holy living, whether it be in our homes, or churches, or other places.

Unfortunately, our definition of *holiness* can bring us into unwanted controversy with Christians who are either more stringent or more liberal than we are. These differences usually center around practices and amusements of a nonreligious nature that fill our lives. As always, our focal point must be on what is the biblical teaching on this matter. Let us look at the broad biblical use of these terms.

Many people regard spirituality and worldliness as a list of do's and don'ts. Unintentionally, by making holiness a matter of rule-keeping, they debase the holiness God requires.

SPECIFIC COMMANDS

The Bible is explicit in laying down, in general, God's will for

Christian behavior. For example, "You shall not murder. You shall not commit adultery. You shall not steal. . . . You shall not covet . . ." (Deuteronomy 5:17-21). Such commands are universal. They are specific. They include all people in all cultures at all times, and they leave no room for doubt or difference of opinion. Those who pray for God's guidance to indulge in one of these activities are wasting their time.

Another example, a less familiar yet very specific command, is found in 2 Corinthians 6:14, "Do not be yoked together with unbelievers." This means, among other things, that a Christian is never to marry an unbeliever. Do you know someone praying about whether or not to marry a non-Christian? You can tell the person, "Save your breath!"

NONSPECIFIC COMMANDS

There are, on the other hand, areas in which God has given no specific instructions. The disagreements among Christians about what is worldly develops over these nonspecific areas that the Bible doesn't spell out—VCRs, cards, movies, dances, rock music, drinking alcohol, ad infinitum. Any list of behavioral practices we would make for ourselves would certainly be blackballed by another group. We would find that most of these taboos were unheard of when the Bible was written, so naturally it is silent about them.

The absence of an explicit biblical standard for many of these debatable items is just the beginning of the problem. Geographical and cultural variations complicate the situation even more. There are parts of the country where it would be unthinkable to appear in church in jeans. In other areas, and in some denominations, no one would dream of excluding someone because of clothing from hearing God's Word. Standards do vary.

When I visited Europe, I discovered that many French Christians drink wine as a matter of course. Their faith doesn't negate this accepted custom. In fact, outside their churches for miles around, the landscape is carpeted with grape vineyards, owned and managed by the Christians. Yet, many groups in our country would roundly condemn a Christian who took even one drink. Some also attach biblical authority to their particular convictions (which may be scripturally justified in their particular situations). From there they generalize and attempt to legislate their own code of behavior for everyone. When strong convictions take hold, they spawn a plethora of new groups for their believers.

What Is Legitimate?

The issue of what is legitimate Christian behavior is no new problem. In the first century, Paul had to set both the Roman and Corinthian Christians straight on this matter. Speaking to the situation in Rome, Paul set down basic principles in Romans 14. He addressed a cosmopolitan church that included Gentile believers—some who had been converted out of pagan idolatry and others who had never worshiped idols. Added to these were the Jewish believers, who cherished a heritage of ceremonies and holy days. In Jesus Christ all these believers had been made one; but their backgrounds and behavioral differences caused clashes and dissension.

One controversy concerned meat. It was meat that had probably been used in idol worship before it wound up in the marketplace. We can assume that the Roman dispute was similar to those in the church at Corinth, described in 1 Corinthians 8:1-13;

10:25-29. Some believers—probably the Jewish Christians—were eating this meat without any qualms. I can imagine them thinking as they entered the meat market, "It's been offered to a worthless idol? So what? Meat is meat, and I like meat."

You see, the Jews disclaimed any involvement in the meat's previous use. But the other believers—former idol worshipers—were scandalized because their brethren ate this meat. Before their conversion, they had eaten the meat as a part of their idol worship. When they forsook the idols, they also forsook the meat. In their own thinking, they couldn't separate the two acts. Naturally, they were bewildered to see a Christian buy and enjoy such meat.

A second controversy plagued the church at Rome. This time it was whether Christians should keep the Jewish holy days and feasts alluded to in Colossians 2:16 as "a religious festival, a New Moon celebration or a Sabbath day." Probably it was the Jewish Christians who couldn't understand the Gentiles' airy disregard for holy days and feasts. For their part, the Gentiles were surprised that a little thing like this should disturb the Jews. Can't you hear them asking, "What's that observance got to do with Christianity anyway? The crux of the matter is Jesus Christ. We've come to know him. You can keep your holy days and feasts if you want them. That's fine with us; suit yourselves. But we can't regard them as inherent in Christianity."

Learning to Deal with Controversy

There was grinding tension on each score, and both groups made the same mistake—they assumed that their customs and culture were the inspired norms of Christianity. Unable to see the other's point of view, they allowed the schism to grow wider.

People drew spiritual conclusions about others' external behavior instead of seeking to understand their inner motivations.

Does any of this seem familiar in your own life or in your group? Christians virtually can be devoured by such controversies, distracted from inner growth in the Lord and cooled toward their fellow believers. Since the entire Christian community faces similar clashes, it's vital that we understand Paul's general principles as he stated them in Romans 14.

1. Don't Judge

Paul states the first principle in Romans 14:3-4, 10-13. "The man who eats everything *must not look down* on him who does not, and the man who does not eat everything *must not condemn* the man who does" (v. 3, emphasis mine).

Paul asked the question, "Who are you to judge someone else's servant?" (v. 4). Then he backed up his argument with immutable fact; God has accepted these people. God alone is our Master and our Judge. We are not entitled to set ourselves up to judge others. If the Scripture is not explicit about some activity, we have no right to criticize or condemn other people because they behave contrary to our opinions.

This principle works in two ways. Let's apply it to a non-controversial activity like putting together jigsaw puzzles. I may feel that I have the liberty to work on a puzzle. This liberty does not give me the right to call the person who refrains an "old fogey." On the other hand, perhaps I don't have the liberty to indulge in this pastime. I can't, therefore, accuse other Christians of being worldly because they sit down with a puzzle.

The Revised Standard Version translates Romans 14:3-4: "Let not him who eats *despise* him who abstains, and let not him who abstains *pass judgment* on him who eats" (emphasis mine). It's our *attitude* toward other Christians that counts here. Ninety percent of the tension over behavioral differences would be eliminated if we could get our attitudes straightened out. Conformity isn't the solution. We don't need to adopt each other's behavioral patterns. But we do need to accept others and realize that they stand or fall before God—not before us. If they dishonor or disobey God, they must answer to him.

2. Let Inner Conviction Mold Behavior

The second principle, which appears in Romans 14:5, emphasizes our own responsibility before God: "One man considers one day more sacred than another; another man considers every day alike. Each one should be fully convinced in his own mind." Personal conviction—not social pressure or some lesser motivation—should mold our behavior. As Christians we desire to honor the Lord Jesus Christ by doing whatever will please and glorify him. And so we base our actions on what we believe to be the will of God for us. This tremendous internal principle will hold in every place, circumstance and occasion.

We can see the meaning of this principle in connection with the training of children. For example, if we try to clamp our children into a mold of do's and don'ts without helping them to understand the whys, they are apt to throw over all our prohibitions as soon as they escape parental supervision. This will happen because they don't understand the *principles* involved.

New Christians are children spiritually. We often try to make them conform to our accustomed behaviors before they've had a chance to discover personally how God is working in their lives. Here's the catch: when they aren't with us, they might abandon our whole behavioral system and revert to their pre-conversion ways.

Are we convinced that our behavior is giving glory to God? This is the first question to ask. When, out of conviction for the Lord's sake, we act or refrain from acting, our choices do not hang on us like a burden; they are a joy. As long as we are convinced before God that we are obeying him, the principle will hold. We do well to consider and reconsider our own behavior in the light of the New Testament to be sure we are following God's will.

3. Celebrate All of Life as from God

The third principle points to the basis for our personal conviction. We read, "If we live, we live to the Lord; and if we die, we die to the Lord. So, whether we live or die, we belong to the Lord" (Romans 14:8).

The totality of our life is to be given over to God for his glory. All of our lives—not just the moments we spend praying, reading the Bible, or witnessing, but the whole of our lives—belongs to God. There are no separate compartments for the sacred and the secular in a Christian's life. You study the Bible to the glory of God. Your game of chess should be equally glorifying to him.

How can anyone play chess to the glory of God? It's simple if we first recognize that our whole lives, every ounce of energy, every moment of time, every dime of money and every other aspect belong to Jesus Christ. We are simply his stewards, and he expects us to invest every part of our lives as being joyfully his. There are times when I ought to be playing chess instead of studying the Bible. There are other times when I should be studying the Bible and not playing chess. This commitment gives us surprising release from unnecessary tension as we live totally in the presence of God with the full intent to honor Jesus Christ.

It's no secret that Christians sometimes have trouble enjoying life. Did you ever have a guilty feeling because you enjoyed a luscious steak that seemed just too delicious or because you spent a great day off with the family? There's no reason to feel guilty. In 1 Timothy 6:17, Paul reminds Timothy of one of Scripture's great facts, that "God . . . richly provides us with everything for our enjoyment." In fact, it is because we are Christians that we can enter more fully than others into every kind of enjoyment. As George Robinson wrote in the hymn "Loved with Everlasting Love":

> Heav'n above is softer blue,
> Earth around is sweeter green!
> Something lives in ev'ry hue
> Christless eyes have never seen.

Instead of clinging to that vaguely uneasy feeling when we're finding something pleasureful, let's enjoy all the things he gives us with thanksgiving and to his glory.

But as the recipients of all God's best, let's welcome the stewardship responsibility which that gives us. Many times, we will need to ask ourselves the question: "Is this activity what I should be spending my time doing right now?" Sometimes we need to be out shoveling snow instead of praying; at other times we ought to forget the snow and fall to our knees. Vital Christianity is not limited to the times of so-called spiritual activity or the days or hours when we're involved in obvious Christian fellowship. Jesus Christ is as real and dynamic at four o'clock Tuesday afternoon in the lab or library, home or office as he is at eleven o'clock Sunday morning in church. He enables us to go through the whole of life in his presence, with him right at our sides. Every aspect, every moment of our lives belongs to God and can glorify him.

Has this concept ever burst through to you? Or do you cling to a compartmentalized existence? If we are mentally sorting the things we do into *spiritual* and *non-spiritual* compartments, this may explain much of our failure to live zestful, through-and-through Christian lives. On the other hand, when we grasp the concept that each moment can be lived in God's will and for his glory, the accumulation of those moments is weighted with eternal significance.

4. Examine Your Motives

The fourth principle appears in Romans 14:14: "I am fully convinced that no food is unclean in itself. But if anyone regards something as unclean, then for him it is unclean."

Many things are not wrong in themselves, but our use of them may be wrong. We just mentioned steak. Food is necessary, but we can misuse food and abuse our bodies through gluttony. Sex, a very wonderful gift of God, becomes one of the most sordid things in life when its function is distorted. In themselves these things are not wrong; the wrong lies in their misuse. External things can become our master; the tail can wag the dog. For this reason Paul is concerned with our attitude toward things. If we believe before God it is wrong for us to indulge in a particular activity but we do so anyway, we are guilty of disobedience. And it doesn't matter if someone else thinks that particular action is right.

The Weak Brother

Involved in our attitude toward a thing must be our concern for the "weak brother." Let's not regard a weak brother simply as a person who isn't strong enough to do what we feel at liberty to do, nor as domineering Christians who want to force their legalistic list of don'ts on everyone. Essentially, weak brothers are Christians who are immature in their thinking. Often they're young Christians who haven't yet learned to distinguish between an act and the motivation behind it. Instead of asking the basic question "Why should(n't) I do that?" weak brothers judge spirituality in terms of external actions. They're probably taking their standards of evaluation wholesale from their family or church group.

God's concern, we must remember, is with our motivation. In Romans 14:6, Paul was really saying that those who eat, eat to glorify the Lord, and those who won't eat abstain to glorify the Lord. Here we have two extremes in behavior, but both are followed to honor the Lord. Weak brothers accept one of these extremes as the right way to act and overlook the motivation that makes it right. If they then see someone following the other extreme, they'll either be offended or confused or both. They need to learn (and so do we all sometimes) that Christians' love for Jesus Christ and their desire to honor and glorify him must always come first. Then what they do or don't do will follow.

So what do we do about weak brothers? Bowl them over and keep rolling? Some of the Roman Christians must have said, "Phooey on weak brothers anyway! They're just immature, so why bother?" Paul wasted no words in reprimanding them: "If your brother is distressed because of what you eat, you are no longer acting in love" (v. 15). We, the supposedly mature Christians who realize the fallacy of basing spiritual judgments on external acts, must be mature enough to accommodate our brethren who still don't understand.

Through the love of God we've got to refuse to trip up or upset a brother on any minor issue. In 1 Corinthians 8—10, Paul elaborates on our responsibility for weaker brothers. (If this subject concerns you, meditate on 8:10-13; 9:19-23; 10:23-33.) Paul himself had personally resolved, "If what I eat causes my brother to fall into sin, I will never eat meat again, so that I will not cause him to fall" (1 Corinthians 8:13). It's the kingdom of God, you see, not our personal liberty that's at stake. And the kingdom of God involves deeper matters than whether we keep a holy day, eat meat or do the twentieth-century equivalents. As Romans 14:17 says, "The kingdom of God is not a matter of eating and drinking, but of righteousness, peace and joy in the Holy Spirit."

It is regrettable but amazing how much thought, discussion, time and energy can be focused on differences of opinion on externals. Subtly we are sidetracked from a positive, outgoing Christian life. Let's determine to avoid this at all costs! When we see a deep spiritual chasm developing, we may need to accommodate ourselves to weak brothers so we can help them to realize what the kingdom means. At the same time, we shouldn't let them get the idea that they can impose their pet behavioral patterns on others. Our counsel may help them toward more mature thinking. This was Paul's purpose in writing to the Roman and Corinthian churches. He helped them to see beyond their immature emphasis on the external act and encouraged them to develop a more permissive and accepting spirit toward Christians whose behavior differed from their own.

I got some practical, firsthand experience with this problem at a student conference in New Jersey some years ago. There I met a fellow, a salesman, who literally had worshiped baseball before he became a Christian. He would slave away all winter long so that he could be completely free for his god in the summer months. For something like twelve years he hadn't missed a single game in Philadelphia. He knew every batting average since 1910. He slept, ate, drank and breathed baseball. Then he met the Savior and gave up his idol, leaving it at Jesus' feet.

Toward the end of our rugged and somewhat exhausting conference, this fellow overheard me suggest to another staff member, "Say, after the conference, let's go over to Connie Mack Stadium and see the Phillies. They're playing the St. Louis Cards." The salesman was staggered. Incredulous, he stared at me and demanded, "How can you as a Christian go to a baseball game?"

Now I've heard a lot of taboos in Christian circles, but this was the first time I'd heard baseball banned! I was flabbergasted and didn't know what to say. Then he asked a second time, "How can you and Fred claim to be Christians and then go out to a ball game?"

Fred and I started thinking through and discussing the situation. As we talked to the salesman, we uncovered his problem. Here was a man like the Gentile Christians in Rome, a former idol worshiper. Baseball had been a big thing to him; now he assumed that anybody who saw a game (ate meat), however removed from idolatrous intents, was worshiping baseball as an idol.

Fred and I canceled our baseball date since our going would have needlessly disturbed our friend at a sensitive stage in his Christian life. But we also talked with him at length and warmly commended his 100-percent commitment to please the Lord.

After awhile I think he realized that not all Christians find baseball a problem. With his background, baseball will probably be a dangerous temptation to him for the rest of his life; this he knew. But later he also saw that he couldn't legislate for Christians who have no problem with the sport. It heartened us to see him begin to mature in his attitudes.

We have a responsibility for our weak brother. The biblical principle does not allow us to go along our way with a willy-nilly attitude, thinking, "They're wrong, they're naive, they won't agree anyway, so I'll just ignore them." Nor does the biblical principle call us to conform to someone else's conscience apart from our own investigating and soul-searching.

Instead, the biblical principle demands that we examine our motives: Am I doing this and not doing that because of love for Jesus Christ and a desire to honor and glorify him? Or is the real reason a cultural bias that won't hold if I move from one social or cultural group to another?

After our motives have been established, we still have to decide what our attitude toward some particular activity should be. This is especially a problem when the position of Scripture isn't explicit.

I think we all realize by now that many secondary issues in Christian behavior fall into a gray area of relativism. What's right for you may be wrong for me. But Paul has some specific advice for us. He draws the line of distinction-doubt:

> I am fully convinced that no food is unclean in itself. But if anyone regards something as unclean, then for him it is unclean. . . . So whatever you believe about these things keep between yourself and God. Blessed is the man who

does not condemn himself by what he approves. But the man who has doubts is condemned if he eats, because his eating is not from faith; and everything that does not come from faith is sin. (Romans 14:14, 22-23)

Once my salesman friend understood the situation, it would have been all right for me to take in the ball game as a recreational exercise. But it would still have been wrong for him to go, for in his case doubt and other moral issues were involved.

A Rule of Thumb

I've found this a very helpful rule of thumb: If there is any doubt about the propriety of some activity, hold off. But if conscience is clear before God and if the thing can be done to his glory, without confusing someone else in the process, do it with pleasure. Rejoice. Be happy about whatever God has given you to enjoy. This is Paul's clear-cut principle.

Some, of course, will always misinterpret and abuse their privilege of personal liberty by taking it as license to do whatever they please. Such behavior negates everything Paul is saying here. I'm always suspicious of those who flaunt their different behavior to show how "free" they are. This is a far cry from holiness. They have missed Paul's tone and intent by a mile.

Love for other Christians is the controlling factor of all that we do when we live the whole of our lives to the glory of God. After the marriage ceremony, a groom doesn't tell his dearly beloved, "Well, now that the commitment's made and the ceremony's over, I'm going out and have a ball. See you later!" The love which draws two people together in the first place is the abiding basis of their marriage. Because they love one another they want to do everything that will please each other. It is painful for them to know they have done something that brings displeasure or harm to the other person. Love constrains them.

Augustine knew what he was saying in his classic statement, "Love God, and do as you please." And he wasn't suggesting compartmentalization. A "my sins are forgiven; now I can live like the devil" attitude offers prima facie evidence that people don't know the love of their heavenly Father and crucified Savior.

An expression of love for the Lord Jesus Christ and a desire to live completely for his glory are evidence of the new life in Christ. When our personal liberty in Christ is directed by this motivation, it is a wonderful freedom—bringing glory to Christ, enjoyment to ourselves, and comfort and edification to others.

WORLDLINESS: AN ATTITUDE OF SELF-INDULGENCE

In the final analysis, worldliness is essentially a self-indulgent attitude. It may take many forms but, more than the exterior series of behavioral patterns, it is an internal attitude. The most common and the most subtle form of worldliness among Christians is probably pride. Some of the most worldly people are safely masqueraded behind their diligent abstinence from doing all the things we usually call "worldly." But they are worldly because their basic concern is themselves, their own comfort, their own prestige, their own material prosperity. Merely abstaining from certain things is no guarantee that we are spiritual.

Genuine spirituality is viewing everything from God's vantage point. His standard of values and his revealed will are what I strive for with all my being. Our attitude and prayer is that everything we say and do may bring glory to Jesus Christ who loves us and gave himself for us.

QUESTIONS FOR INDIVIDUAL OR GROUP STUDY

1. In the preceding century, a Christian college made this boast in their catalog, "Located sixty miles from any known form of sin." In that case, the campus must have been more than isolated—it must have been uninhabited! If isolating ourselves from non-Christians doesn't solve the sin problem, why do some Christians do it?

2. Paul Little states, "The Christians in Corinth needed to realize, as we do, that withdrawal from those who do not know Jesus Christ is outright disobedience to the will of the Lord" (p. 175). What did Jesus want us to do instead? Why?

3. What is the difference between *isolation* and *separation?*

4. Christians usually have a harder time handling the moral differences of other Christians than the differences they have with non-Christians. How does this aspect of the chapter relate to our being ambassadors for Christ?

5. Romans 14:1-4 implies that Christians were never meant to have a completely uniform code of conduct when it comes to secondary matters. However, what actions and attitudes does the apostle Paul say hold for all Christians?

6. In what activities might others consider you "the weak brother"? When are you "the strong brother"?

7. To gain some practice determining how you would handle certain "gray areas," decide how you would act in the following case studies. Allow the following questions to guide you:
   - What would you do in this situation?
   - How would you feel if a Christian friend criticized your action?
   - If a Christian friend were in this situation and did the op-

posite of what you would do, how would you feel and
what should you do?

Case Study One: We can survive without a new stereo, but it
would certainly enhance the beauty and comfort of our home.
I know we can always send the money to missionaries or give
it to our church. Can I feel right about buying a new stereo?

Case Study Two: I've *got* to do my homework on Sunday. We
always get heavier assignments over the weekend and my Sat-
urdays are tied up with church service. I'm not dishonoring
God by doing homework after church on Sunday, am I?

Case Study Three: My best friend is really upset because I
won't boycott a store that he says sells pornography. (It also
happens to have the cheapest prices in town.) He says that
if the whole community doesn't band together nothing will
get done. Should I boycott my favorite discount store? Will
it ruin my witness to him if I don't?

8. Paul Little offers this rule of thumb: "If there is any doubt
about the propriety of some activity, hold off. But if conscience is clear before God and if the thing can be done to
his glory, without confusing someone else in the process, do
it with pleasure." Is there a situation in which you should
put this advice to work this week?

SUGGESTIONS FOR A STUDY-GROUP LEADER

1. Allow group members to share how they applied last week's
study. You may want to discuss why they succeeded or failed
to carry out their personal applications.

2. Find out if the group would like to discuss some situations
they have actually faced. You could analyze the dilemmas by
answering the same questions given in question seven.

9

Living by Faith

Faith is the key to maintaining a
real Christian experience. We accept the doctrine that we are
saved by faith: through faith alone we come to Jesus Christ and
invite him into our lives as Lord and Savior. But we easily forget
that faith must continue as the operating principle in our Christian lives from day to day.

We're apt to pull a switch in our thinking—an unconscious
switch, perhaps, but a devastating one. After starting the Christian
life by faith we try to live it by works. Although we know that salvation can't be earned by works, sometimes we imagine that we
must work out the Christian life by doing certain things. This idea
is false. The same faith that introduces us to life in Jesus Christ
must continue to operate throughout our Christian lives. The object of our faith also remains the same: Jesus Christ the Lord.

DESIRE CHRIST, NOT A PACKAGE
Scripture points us clearly to Jesus as the constant object of our

faith. I like the Revised Standard Version's translation of 1 Corinthians 1:30, where Paul reminds us, "He [God] is the source of your life in Christ Jesus, whom God made our wisdom, our righteousness and sanctification and redemption." Jesus Christ is to be our wisdom; he is our righteousness, sanctification, redemption. Peter makes a more staggering statement about our Lord in 2 Peter 1:3, "His divine power has given us everything we need for life and godliness through our knowledge of him [Jesus Christ]."

Did you catch that? Because we know Jesus (who has called us by his grace) we have all things that we need for life and godliness. He's given them to us because of his divine grace. Do you realize that because you have received Jesus Christ into your life as Savior and Lord, right now you have *everything necessary* for a life of godliness and holiness?

Most of us tend to ask God for little packages—I know I do. We'll say, "Lord, I need more love" or "I need more joy, Lord. And I need more peace of mind too." We need more of this and more of that. But God doesn't supply us with a packet of love or joy or peace. If he did, we would be foolish enough to think of them as our own achievements and go around boasting, "See how I love people. Just look at the power in my life. Don't overlook my peace of mind, either." No, God knows better. He has given you and me everything we need in the Lord Jesus Christ.

Once we've received him into our lives and have established a personal relationship with him, we have all that God is going to give us. Absolutely everything that we need at this moment is in Jesus Christ—ours to appropriate, if we will. And Jesus Christ is living within us! As we pray in faith to him each day, he will impart everything he sees necessary for us.

But how does this theoretical statement become practical? How do we seek the Lord by faith, and then experience the reality of faith? What are the necessary ingredients that should always characterize our Christian lives, and how can we maintain that genuine faith in Jesus Christ?

IS GOD'S VOICE AUDIBLE?

To start with, we have to know what we're looking for. We've all run into non-Christians who say, "I'd believe in God if you could prove him to me." When I've asked them "What would you accept as proof?" they're staggered. They have never stopped to think about what they're looking for. They wouldn't recognize the evidence if they stumbled over it.

In our personal contact with God, we may share their problem. We're a little hazy about what we're after. Are we waiting for someone else's experience—maybe a voice from heaven? A friend may have told us, "God spoke to me . . ." and we exclaimed, "That's tremendous!" But then we began thinking about ourselves: "God never speaks to me. I wonder why I've never heard voices. Maybe there's something wrong with me."

It's easy to misunderstand others' expressions. Then we get confused, and without knowing quite what we're looking for, we try to duplicate their experiences. When we think we have to have a great ecstatic experience that will set us turning cartwheels or spinning like a top, our ideas about the reality of faith get all out of kilter. Soon we begin to get frustrated.

I don't hear an audible voice when God speaks to me. I hear his Word. Reading in your Bible morning after morning, do you ever sense that a particular passage is God's message to you for that day? Have you ever felt that God is saying something directly to you through his Word? Have you ever known the peace of Jesus Christ in a crisis? These are all examples of personal contact with God.

Can you find anything about your life that's different because Jesus Christ is in it? That difference is a result of a genuine relationship with God. Stop a minute and ask yourself where you would be today if you had never encountered Jesus Christ. You may discover that there is more objective evidence of the work of Jesus Christ in your life than you'd thought.

By faith we know the reality of Jesus Christ. By faith we find him more real to us than a close member of our own family. By faith we can "practice his presence"; that is, we can learn to think of him as a person continually present with us. Omnipresence, of course, is an attribute of God. It is a fact about God that Christians accept—but few act on. We can train ourselves to think of him in concrete situations, to be conscious that he is with us here and now, to remember that his resources are always available to us. If we do so, we will find him an inexhaustible source of all we need.

TEMPTATIONS

Jesus Christ, himself, is all we need. Suppose you're in a tense situation, tempted to blow your stack. You can't stand that roommate another minute. What do you do? This very moment you can turn to Jesus Christ in faith and say, "Lord, I can't love this clod. I don't have what it takes. Only your love will do. Love him through me." Recognizing your lack, you come to Jesus Christ by faith at the moment of need.

For some of us the word *temptation* suggests only one thing: sexual impurity. Sexual impurity certainly is a temptation to reckon with, but all kinds of other things tempt us too, such as the urge to backbite or slay with sarcasm. Christians seem to be susceptible to the sins of the spirit far more than to wrong external acts. We can afford to be less concerned about the many external temptations that don't bother us, but we need to be more alert for the internal temptations that come up all the time. The Lord is waiting to hear us pray, "Lord, I need your patience because I'm impatient. The pressures are getting me down, and I don't have it in me to fight them. Thank you that you live in me and that you're willing to release your patience. Please do so in my life now."

Temptations in our thought life must be nailed at the outset. I'm sure you've heard this old adage, but it bears repetition: "You can't stop the birds from flying over your head, but you can keep them from building a nest in your hair." Just as soon as we're tempted with an unclean thought, or an unjust or malicious one, we need to turn to Jesus Christ and say, "Lord, I don't have the power to beat this thing. Inside me is a wretched response to evil. But *you* have the power. I'm turning to you to release your power in my life."

Instead of looking to Jesus for victory, some of us have tried to battle the temptation itself. This is what defeats us. Suppose I say, "Don't think about white elephants for the next five minutes." Try as you will, you'll never succeed. Inherent in trying not to think about white elephants is a concentration on them.

We need to look past the tempting situation and see Jesus. "Lord, you are the source of love. I can't love this person (I almost despise him); but you do. Help me." Jesus Christ is all we need. Instead of more packages of love, peace, purity or power, he offers us himself, a living person. What do we honestly think of his offer?

What is Jesus Christ to us? Is he simply a series of facts on a piece of paper or is he a living person? Whether we realize it or not, Jesus Christ is living within you through the Holy Spirit. If you don't realize it, then he's obviously going to be meaningless to you. It's a revolutionary experience to have the truth burst upon you that he is alive. The life of faith day by day is just a continuing recognition of the risen, living Lord.

NOT STRIVING, BUT LOOKING

We're defeated sometimes because we spend too much time worrying about whether our faith is strong enough. Satan has us working from the wrong end of the stick. Hudson Taylor had to learn this truth, and so do we. He described his (and our) plight in one of his letters: "All the time I felt assured that there was in Christ all I needed, but the practical question was—how to get it out.... I saw that faith was the only requisite . . . but I had not this faith."[1] One day he received a letter from a friend which pointed out the solution: "But how to get faith strengthened? Not by striving after faith, but by resting on the Faithful One,"[2] "by looking off to the Faithful One."[3]

Not faith itself but the object of our faith requires our attention. We should never be absorbed with our faith, disregarding the object that determines it. Look to Jesus Christ. Someone has said that strong faith in a weak plank will land you in the river, but weak faith in a strong plank will get you across.

Faith lays hold of the "givens" in the Christian life and lives in the light of them. It's not always easy to do. Depression hits; you feel miserable. How can you get out of the dumps? Not by dwelling on your depression and all the things that have gone wrong. Sit down and ponder, instead, the amazing facts about Jesus Christ: who he is, what he has done in history, what he has done in your own life. Think of him now as the great High Priest, appearing in the presence of God for you—compassionate, able to save you to the uttermost. Allow yourself to meditate about him for ten or fifteen minutes, and involuntarily you'll find yourself singing.

Daily personal fellowship with the living God is vital. When we haven't been alone in God's presence for a while, we have trouble thinking of anything except our problems. Try this now. Meditate on what God has done in Jesus Christ and how he is God's gift to you. You'll find him lifting you out of yourself.

The prayers of the Bible follow this basic pattern: people remind themselves of who God is and of all he has done and then they pray about their own situations. They may start with creation and then recall what God did with Israel or Elijah. After gaining momentum and confidence they pray, "Now, Lord, here we are. Give us courage and wisdom for the present situation."

We need to remind ourselves of God's mercies in our own lives. Christians have short memories when it comes to their experiences with God. Recalling what God has done in the past increases our confidence in the face of present problems. I believe such concrete reminders of God's love, wisdom and power are the shield of faith which the apostle Paul in Ephesians 6:16 exhorts us to take to quench all the flaming darts of the evil one. What are his darts? Not only obvious, overt sins, but the secret fantasizing, fears and doubts known only to us.

GOD'S IN CHARGE

Faith recognizes that God is in control of my life and understands every harrowing mess I get into. Whether I believe it or not, it's a fact that God is also in control of the world. If I don't believe it, I'm just robbing myself of the enjoyment of the fact. But if I meditate on this fact and lay hold of it, my fears about the future seem unfounded.

Experience proves this. A lot of my traveling from campus to campus is by air. Just before I'm scheduled to fly somewhere, my wife usually hears about several recent plane crashes. Such news never reassures us. In fact, I would probably cancel my flight if I didn't have the confidence that my life is in God's hand, that my family is also in his hand and that nothing will happen in our lives by accident. Some people who have no assurance about their future really sweat it out during a plane flight. God has helped me to remain at peace in such times. You see, people either have faith in God's care or they don't. The statement that God is in control is either true or it's not true. If it's not true, we'd better forget about God. But if it is true and we accept God's revelation of himself, our faith enables us to enjoy and rest in the certainty of his providence.

Faith gives our lives an amazingly new perspective. Faith acknowledges God's sovereign control but is not fatalistic. Fatalism submits to a blind, impersonal force over which people have no control. Faith in the providence of God yields willingly to a loving heavenly Father, who sees the two sparrows that fall to the ground and who numbers the hairs of each head. Faith is a far cry from fatalism, and in that difference there is great comfort.

Faith encounters many challenges. Dr. Edward Carnell likens the Christian to a physicist watching a magic show. Each successful trick threatens the physicist's faith in the law of uniformity. He may admittedly be baffled, but his faith is not overthrown because he knows that the law of uniformity depends on scientific rather than private grounds.

Similarly, Christians' faith is strengthened as they keep the promises of God before them and consider, not "the difficulties in the way of the things promised, but the character and resources of God who has made the promise."[4] (See Romans 4:20.) Job did just this in response to his wife's taunts when God seemed to have abandoned him to incredible suffering. She told him not to be an idiot—to curse God and die! But Job declared, "Though he slay me, yet will I hope in him" (Job 13:15).

Habakkuk was bewildered by the events of his day. Judah lay in moral ruin, but God wasn't judging the people. When the prophet asked, "How come?" the Lord answered him, "I'm going to use Chaldea to chastise them." Habakkuk found it even harder to swallow *that* explanation, for Chaldea was more wicked than Judah.

Habakkuk had to learn to take the long view of God in his dealing with people. Only then could he confidently affirm that even without any external manifestation of God's presence and power, yet he would trust him. He said, "Though the fig tree does not bud and there are no grapes on the vines . . . yet I will rejoice in the LORD, I will be joyful in God my Savior" (Habakkuk 3:17-18). We see faith here, not wishful thinking. Faith recognizes the realities that have now been revealed in the Lord Jesus Christ; faith takes hold of them and lives in their light.

DAILY FAITH

Living by faith is a day-by-day experience. Yesterday's leftover manna cannot satisfy us today. We must continue in God's presence every day. There's no debate about this. It is a simple, but profound fact—and a crucial one in our lives with God.

Perhaps you've heard of George Mueller, the founder of orphanages in England, who as a man of faith never made a public announcement of his needs but depended on God to provide for every necessity. George Mueller's life taught me a valuable and a comforting lesson about daily fellowship with God. You see, I used to have the idea that once Christians had it, whatever *it* was, all their problems would be ended. They'd always see the beaming sunlight, hear the birds twittering and feel like turning cartwheels for joy. But even George Mueller admitted, "I consider it my greatest need before God and man to get my soul happy before the Lord each day before I see anybody."

George Mueller's key word was *get*. His soul wasn't always happy when he woke up. He must have felt just as I do when the alarm clock sounds. You know that cold-mashed-potatoes feeling that comes when you wake up and begin to remember all your problems? I'm sure he knew this feeling. As the day's first task, Mueller got himself into the presence of God to meditate on him until his soul became happy in the Lord. Then he faced the day.

The Christian life isn't an entirely passive affair. I prefer a description like *victorious battle* to *victorious life* because the latter is apt to leave the false impression that Christians have no problems. There are definitely struggles; we too live in the real world. My reading of the New Testament and my own experience have confirmed this. Life is a battle, but it is a great, victorious battle when by faith we daily trust the God of Habakkuk, George Mueller and others who never lost sight of God's character and faithfulness and who willingly fought God's battles.

I think that sometimes we've made the "victorious Christian life," or "being filled with the Holy Spirit," or whatever you want to call it, far too complicated. Some people may call me naive, but I've read every book I can find on the subject and listened to dozens of talks. There are plenty of formulas out there. As I've read the New Testament and talked to others, I've concluded—and I'm open to correction—that, call it what you will, the key is being totally sold out, without reservation, to Jesus Christ.

The reality of such faith carries us through all of life's ups and downs. Sometimes we feel emotional about the Lord Jesus; at other times we don't. This is healthy. People couldn't last long at a high-fever pitch of emotion; they'd wear out. Imagine what it would be like to constantly live at the emotional level you hit during the last seconds of a tied (your team has the ball) championship basketball game. We have our moments of intense emotion, but then our feelings undulate. But whether we feel high, low or just pretty levelheaded, underneath we can know the reality of Jesus Christ and his gift of pervading peace and contentment.

Knowing Jesus Christ we're no longer tied to circumstances. We don't bob up and down at their command. Instead, we're tied to the living and unchanging God. We can step over circumstances as long as we know we are trusting him and actively receiving his life and allowing him to work it out in us. With this kind of faith, the apostle Paul was able to sing in prison.

Don't kid yourself about Paul. He didn't get a kick out of living in prison or receiving the thirty-nine lashes. Such hardships were as devastating for him as they would be for us. With Jesus Christ, though, he had found what enabled him to transcend his circumstances. Depending on the life of Christ in him, Paul's life was a genuine experience of faith.

A hymn that expresses well the reality of living by faith in all life's situations is based on the promise of Jesus' continuing presence. He said, "Never will I leave you; never will I forsake you" (Hebrews 13:5); "And surely I am with you always, to the very end of the age" (Matthew 28:20). As we lay hold of this basic promise and live in its light, we can share in the genuine life of faith which this writer affirms:

> I take Thy promise, Lord, in all its length,
> And breadth and fulness, as my daily strength,
> Into life's future fearless I may gaze,
> For, Jesus, Thou art with me all the days.
>
> There may be days of darkness and distress,
> When sin has power to tempt, and care to press;
> Yet in the darkest day I will not fear,
> For, 'mid the shadows, Thou wilt still be near.
>
> Days there may be of joy, and deep delight,
> When earth seems fairest, and her skies most bright;
> Then draw me closer to Thee, lest I rest
> Elsewhere, my Savior, than upon Thy breast.
>
> And all the other days that make my life,
> Mark'd by no special joy or grief or strife,
> Days fill'd with quiet duties, trivial care,
> Burdens too small for other hearts to share,

Spend Thou these days with me, all shall be Thine
So shall the darkest hour with glory shine.
Then when these earthly years have pass'd away,
Let me be with Thee in the perfect day.[5]

QUESTIONS FOR INDIVIDUAL OR GROUP STUDY

1. Paul Little describes the Christian life as a "victorious battle"
   rather than a victorious life. It is true most of us fail our Lord
   time and time again. If this is your situation, how did it color
   your reading of the chapter?

2. Why do you think Little includes a chapter on faith in a
   book on witnessing?

3. "We're apt to pull a switch in our thinking—an unconscious
   switch, perhaps, but a devastating one. After starting the
   Christian life by faith we try to live it by works" (p. 192).
   Why is living by works more attractive than living by faith?

4. How would you define *faith* in light of the entirety of Hebrews 11?

5. One definition of *faith* is "envisioning what God wants to accomplish in a situation and acting within his plans." How
   did Abraham (Hebrews 11:8-10), Moses' parents (v. 23) and
   Rahab (v. 31) live out this definition of faith?

6. The author points out that "Most of us tend to ask God for little packages. . . . But God doesn't supply us with a packet of
   love or joy or peace. . . . He has given you and me everything
   we need in the Lord Jesus Christ" (p. 193). How can it be that
   having Jesus Christ in your life will meet every need?

7. Where would you be today if you had never encountered
   Jesus Christ? How could this be seen as objective evidence

that Jesus Christ is at work in your life?

8. Paul Little says, "Not faith itself but the object of our faith requires our attention" (p. 197). "The life of faith day by day is just a continuing recognition of the risen, living Lord" (p. 197). How would such an awareness shape your attitude and actions in the following situations?

- You're staying at a motel with an X-rated movie channel on every TV.

- Your boss is acting obnoxiously at a business lunch you are hosting for a client.

- The child you are baby-sitting for simply won't go to sleep!

- You're dating someone who keeps testing the limits of your sexual boundaries.

9. The author suggests that, "Recalling what God has done in the past increases our confidence in the face of present problems" (p. 198). Read Philippians 4:6-7. The Living Bible phrases it this way: "Don't worry about anything; instead, pray about everything; tell God your needs and don't forget to thank him for his answers. If you do this you will experience God's peace." Take a moment now to thank God for a *similar answer* in the past before asking him to meet a *current need.* Do you have a greater than usual sense that God knows your needs and cares about them? Consider carrying out this principle throughout the next week.

10. How does *faith* differ from *fatalism* (p. 199)? Why is this distinction important?

11. Why do God's answers sometimes differ from what we suggest to him?

Suggestions for a Study-Group Leader

1. Allow group members to share how they applied last week's study. You may want to discuss why they succeeded or failed to carry out their applications.

2. Be prepared to respond to a variety of answers to question one. Some people may need encouragement; others, a warning (see pp. 120-21).

10

Feeding the Spring

———— ❧ ————

Character, someone has said, is what you do when nobody sees you. But most of us are more concerned with what others see. We concentrate on what we say and do in social situations, the kind of impression we want to leave; we don't worry about our thoughts and actions when we're alone. Yet it's then that our true characters come out. We let our hair down and put our feet up on the table. We're really ourselves.

In his helpful and penetrating book *The Meaning of Persons*, Dr. Paul Tournier comments on the disparity between what we are inside and what we appear to be to other people. He calls this disparity the difference between the *person* and the *personage*. Under most circumstances our degree of mental health will be greater if what we appear to be closely approaches what we actually are. The further apart our persons and our personages are, the greater will be our problems in mental health, for a part of our lives will be a lie.

The Secret Self

Throughout Scripture, God has emphasized that our real selves
are the inner or secret selves, the character that emerges when
we're all alone. And God knows everything about our inner
selves. He reminded Samuel of the significance of the inner life
when he sent him to anoint a son of Jesse as king. Samuel
thought that tall, handsome Eliab had everything, until the
Lord told him, "Do not consider his appearance or his height,
for I have rejected him. The Lord does not look at the things
man looks at. Man looks at the outward appearance, but the
Lord looks at the heart" (1 Samuel 16:7). Our hearts, our inner
lives—those centers of our personalities that include intellect,
emotion and will—are the basis for God's evaluation of us. And
the writer to the Hebrews affirms all these facts: "Nothing in all
creation is hidden from God's sight. Everything is uncovered
and laid bare before the eyes of him to whom we must give account" (4:13).

These are some of the most encouraging and the most
frightening words in the Bible. They assure us that God always
understands. Our very best friends will sometimes misunderstand. Often unintentionally, they may misinterpret a word or
motive, and sadness follows. But God knows the whole truth. We
can confide in him because he knows us through and through.
This very fact means, though, that we can't put up a front with
him. At times it's frightening to realize that he knows everything
I know about myself, and more than I know. The living God sees
me as I am when I'm all alone—stripped of all pretense.

We should consider our secret lives, which no one but God
sees, from both a negative and a positive perspective. Moses
speaks of the negative aspect in Psalm 90:8, "You have set our

iniquities before you, our secret sins in the light of your presence." This statement reveals at least three important facts.

1. We all have secret sins.

Moses specifically says *our* iniquities, *our* secret sins. He excludes no one. For some of us, our secret sin may be hidden pride, which through self-inflation makes us see ourselves as better, smarter, kinder, more attractive and more important than we are. It may be self-deception, which encourages us to rationalize our behavior so that we have "justifiable gripes," "understandable frustration," "righteous indignation."

It may be dishonesty, which conceals half the truth or intentionally acts or speaks to create a false impression. It may be selfish hurry, careless waste of time or talents or failure to love as God loves us. It may be wanting anyone or anything outside of God's will for us. It may be bitterness or animosity toward others that is eating us, destroying us as the worm bored through Jonah's gourd. It may be cheating or impurity. But whatever it is, God knows all about our sins. We can't hide it from him. Instead, in his presence we need to acknowledge and come to grips with our hidden sins.

2. Secret sin eventually leads to outward sin.

Open sins are the fruits which grow from the root of secret sin, often sins of motive. That frightens me. Our Lord dealt with this critical condition when he tried to explain to the Pharisees that sin is not necessarily external. Essentially, he said, "You don't understand. It's not what goes into people that defiles them; it's not what others see those people doing or not doing. It's from within, out of people's hearts, that evil thoughts, impurities and all these other things come. People are defiled from within" (see Mark 7:14-23).

Secret sin known only to us always precedes outward sin which is apparent to others. James makes this point: "Each one is tempted when, by his own evil desire, he is dragged away and enticed. Then, after desire has conceived, it gives birth to sin; and sin, when it is full-grown, gives birth to death" (James 1:14-15). Throughout the Bible we find examples: Achan's theft was preceded by a greedy heart. David's adultery began in his imagination. Ananias and Sapphira were only revealing their inner deceit when they lied to God. In each instance the sin existed within the person long before an external deed manifested it.

Did you know that collapse in the Christian life is never a blow-out? It is always a slow leak. Perhaps we make a cutting remark about someone—that's outward; but an uncleansed disposition lies behind it. Whatever sin we may mention can be traced back to a faulty inner attitude, a secret sin. I wonder if there are any slow leaks in my life or yours right now.

3. We must realize that all our secret sins are before God.

If we have any, he sees them, even though we may not be aware of them ourselves. If we are personally unaware of sin, we can open our hearts and minds to God and ask him to show us whether there are secret sins in our lives. We can depend on him to answer!

David's prayer is the place to begin. "Search me, O God, and know my heart; test me and know my anxious thoughts. See if there is any offensive way in me, and lead me in the way everlasting" (Psalm 139:23-24). We can be certain that the Holy Spirit will open our eyes to any sin which he sees in our lives. He may reveal it to us through a passage of Scripture we're meditating on, or he may use someone else's remark to trigger our awareness of it. One way or another, he will always put his finger on the sin to enhance the process of developing our holiness.

Once it's been revealed, it's up to us to come to grips with that particular sin. God never reveals sin to us to leave us in it. He wants us to respond to his revelation by confessing and forsaking that particular sin and by making restitution if it is necessary. He is always ready to hear our requests for forgiveness, cleansing and power.

Satan, on the other hand, doesn't want us to deal with newly discovered sin or repeated sin. And he delights in taunting us by saying, "Not again! You don't have the gall to go back to God and confess this same sin again, do you? You just finished confessing that sin the other day, and you promised you'd forsake it. How can you face him now? You'd better improve your batting average first. Show him that you've got the will power to lick it once and for all."

These words never come from the Lord Jesus. God wants us to come to him immediately, just as we are. Only he can deal with us and our sins. He knew exactly what we were like when he redeemed us in Jesus Christ on the cross. As the illuminating work of the Holy Spirit makes our sin apparent to us, he calls us to come just as we are—without one plea except the blood which the Lord Jesus shed for us.

If the Holy Spirit doesn't reveal any specific sin in our lives after we have asked him to, we don't need to agitate ourselves. The enemy loves to paralyze us and prevent us from effective service. He would even suggest that we are guilty of some unknown sin which God hasn't revealed to us. Satan hopes that instead of resting in God's peace and rejoicing in past and present cleansing and forgiveness, we'll grow introspective. If we become absorbed with ourselves, we'll forget both the Lord and others.

Our Father wants us to recognize that our capacity for sin, and for self-deception concerning sin, is virtually limitless. Jeremiah the prophet pointed out that the heart is deceitful above all things and desperately wicked (Jeremiah 17:9). Yet we can rely on the Savior who keeps on saving and who takes the responsibility for revealing specific sins to us. Thus he relieves us of anxiety and constant self-concern. We can focus our minds on the Lord Jesus Christ, the solution for every sin problem, with a kind of carefree, relaxed trust that should characterize the child of God.

Robert Murray McCheyne struck a good balance when he advised, "For every look you take at yourself, take ten at Jesus Christ." We don't want to be morbidly introspective, like people who take their spiritual temperatures every three days or every three hours. Sometimes we treat our spiritual lives like the little boy who planted a lima bean and then dug it up every morning to see how it was growing. It is through committing every area of our lives to God and then in trusting him that we grow in the personal fellowship with God for which we were intended.

GUARD AND DEVELOP YOUR INNER LIFE

Because of the impact which our inner lives have in determining our outward lives, the Scripture explicitly admonishes us to guard those inner lives: "Above all else, guard your heart, for it is the wellspring of life" (Proverbs 4:23). We are in large part determined by our inner lives. Someone has observed that circumstances never make or break anyone; they simply reveal the person. We are a day-by-day accumulation of everything that has constituted our lives until this point in time—especially of what we have thought, felt and willed.

This is why the psalmist says, "Surely you desire truth in the inner parts; you teach me wisdom in the inmost place" (Psalm 51:6). Here we move from the negative to the positive aspect of our secret lives, personal fellowship with God himself. In James 4:8 we read, "Come near to God and he will come near to you. Wash your hands, you sinners, and purify your hearts, you double-minded." Although ultimately we depend on God alone to redeem and cleanse us, he gives us a positive, active role to take in the process.

This positive aspect of our inner lives of seeking the Lord may be even more influential than the inner searching for impurity. In the Sermon on the Mount, Jesus taught, "When you pray, go into your room, close the door and pray to your Father, who is unseen. Then your Father, who sees what is done in secret, will reward you" (Matthew 6:6). Secret prayer will receive an evident reward from the Father. Our secret lives with God are the root of outward spiritual power, just as secret sin is the root of outward sin. Both are inexorable spiritual laws.

Incredible as it is, the God of creation, who made heaven and earth and us, wants to have personal fellowship with each one of us. What a tremendous fact to lay hold of! We can scarcely grasp its import. Throughout Scripture we see evidence of people in this intimate relationship with the Lord. David affirmed, "In the morning, O LORD, you hear my voice" (Psalm 5:3). Three times a day Daniel bowed down toward Jerusalem to commune with the living God, and then he faced the consequences—lions. After a long and busy day, our Lord rose before daybreak and went out to a lonely place to be alone with his Father.

God enjoys the worship, praise and fellowship of a group of believers gathered in the name of Christ. He is pleased to meet us in chapel, church and prayer groups. But he also likes to meet us alone. As a parent and husband, I love times spent together with the whole family because I love my wife and each of our children. But I treasure time spent alone with my wife or my child. During those times, I get to know the person in a special way. We can confide in each other in a way that is difficult in a group. How sad I would feel if a family member did not want to spend any time alone with me! But that's just the way God must feel about some of us. Of course we spend time with him in certain groups, yet he longs to meet us as individuals.

Now suppose that you wanted to give your parents a special gift. To buy it you had to spend all your time working; you never got home. How would they feel? When they couldn't stand it any longer, wouldn't they burst out, "Look, we don't want your gift; we want you! We'd like a little time with you." It is easy to get so involved "serving the Lord" that we never have any time to spend alone with him. Yet it is those hours alone with him that are essential to a life that possesses spiritual power.

What happens when we meet with God alone? What is necessary if that secret time with the living God is to result in manifest spiritual power? He, of course, speaks to us through his Word, and we respond to him in prayer. Yet sometimes our Bible reading or praying leaves us unsatisfied. What goes wrong?

BIBLE STUDY

In studying the Bible many people seek to discover facts about the Bible, even facts within the Bible. But information about the written Word is not an end in itself. If you've ever tried to produce spiritual life and power simply by reading verses, organizing information and making outlines, you know it's a futile effort. Benjamin Franklin wrote commentaries on the Bible, but as far as we know he never became a Christian.

Basically, the Bible's purpose is to bring us into contact with the living God in Jesus Christ; as one hymn writer put it, "Beyond the sacred page we seek Thee, Lord." A telescope helps to point us to the star. Of course we should know how the telescope works to use it, but what a tragedy when we get engrossed in its operation and forget to look for the star. Failure to distinguish between the means and the end may be the problem a lot of us have in our personal devotions.

Maybe we're thinking, "I've tried a regular quiet time, but it was dry as dust. I couldn't get anything out of it." Have you ever felt as though you were cranking out ten verses a day, like a Buddhist spinning his prayer wheel, and it didn't mean a thing to you? You began to feel discouraged: "What's the use? Why bother?" Very similar feelings hit most of us at times. There's no sense in acting out empty rituals. Maybe we've failed to recognize that the purpose of our quiet times is to come face to face with the living God himself in the Lord Jesus Christ. Or maybe we've failed to realize that he is a living person who wants to meet us. We should always come to the Scripture expecting to meet the living Lord, for essentially his Word is not a textbook but a revelation of himself.

Another problem we may experience in our personal Bible study arises from lack of direction. It's been said, "He who aims at nothing is sure to hit it." If we enter our quiet times with the purpose of getting something to remember, it will help to have a notebook and pen to write down new thoughts. I always keep a col-

umn of specific ways I can apply a truth. Sometimes I write down
a prayer so that I can ask the Lord how to apply it. I've found that
written prayers have fewer requests and far more worship in them.
Lack of purpose will soon depress the appetite for Bible study.

Seven directive questions have helped me immensely as I've
used them from time to time in my own Bible reading. I tried
them when I was just beginning to meet with God every morning, and I still refer to them occasionally, especially if the approach I'm currently using starts to go stale on me. If you come
to the Word of God prayerfully and search the passage for answers to each question, you'll discover pertinent applications
every time. A few of the seven questions may not fit a particular
passage, but others will. Some apply to every passage. Although
simple, these questions can keep us from whizzing through a
string of verses with our mind on today's schedule or yesterday's
events. They arrest our flights of thought and bring us face to
face with the living God and his will.

1. Is there an example for me to follow?
Does this passage of Scripture suggest anything that I should do
or be today? Instead of reading Scripture as an academic exercise, we should always consider God's truth with the intent to
pattern our lives according to his revealed will.

2. Is there a sin for me to avoid?
It's easy to see situations in Scripture that apply to other people.
The hard thing is recognizing parallels to sins in our own lives!

3. Is there a command for me to obey?
We often wonder about God's will for our lives. And we often

talk as though discerning God's will for us were a difficult and perplexing problem. Do you realize that 95 percent of his will has already been revealed? This can be a shattering discovery. God has revealed his will in the Bible. In our long, impressive prayers about seeking the will of God, we're usually thinking in terms of marriage or a career. But from one point of view these two decisions are incidental. God clearly states his will for our character and daily life. Sometimes we don't know his will for one reason only: We haven't exposed ourselves to the Word of God to look for it.

Is there a command to obey? If—as so often happens—we have been disobedient about something God has made clear, we can't expect him to disclose more of his will to us. First he expects us to obey what he has shown us, for his declared will is not optional to us. God reveals his will to us progressively, according to our obedience.

4. Is there a promise for me to claim?

Is the Holy Spirit directing me through this passage of Scripture to a promise which I can now possess by faith? Some promises in Scripture, like Hebrews 13:5, are unconditional: "Never will I leave you; never will I forsake you." Others have a condition attached to them, "Delight yourself in the LORD and he will give you the desires of your heart" (Psalm 37:4). As we search for the promises, we need to see and think through their conditions too, and then claim them accordingly.

5. What does this particular passage teach about God or about Jesus Christ?

The adventure of the Christian life in many ways resembles

marriage. No engaged couple really knows each other. Although each person has tried to discover as much as possible about the prospective partner, by the couple's first wedding anniversary they'll look back and say, "I didn't know you when I married you, and I don't think you knew me." This, parenthetically, is reason enough for me to shudder at the thought of any marriage that lacks the certainty of God's will. You don't really know the other person beforehand. The process of getting to know one's partner is one of the great adventures of marriage.

Similarly, one of the adventures of the Christian life is growing in our personal knowledge of the Lord Jesus Christ. At the outset we know a few things about him, enough to commit our lives to him and receive him into our lives as Lord and Savior. We trust him. We agree to be totally obedient. Yet we scarcely know him. By meditating on his own revelation of himself and by growing in him, we get to know God better and better. Then as life goes on, through our own personal experiences with him, he gives added dimensions to a fact we have already learned about him in Scripture; that is to say, that God is merciful, that God honors his word.

6. Is there a difficulty here for me to explore?

Some people always look for the questions first, only to get swamped by problems and difficulties. Before long they make the excuse, "There are so many things I don't understand. I can't make head nor tail out of them; it's no use even to try." When we eat fish, most of us set aside the bones so we can eat the fish itself. But a few concentrate on the bones and never get to the fish. Whether eating fish or studying the Bible, bone-picking does not satisfy. We should jot down questions that puzzle us and then look for their answers later. But we shouldn't make the problems the main course of our meal.

7. Is there something in this passage that I should pray about today?

Some of us have trouble with prayer. Every day seems the same—nothing more than a repetition of yesterday's words, "O Lord, bless me and Mom and Mary and the whole world, for Jesus' sake, Amen." If we're alert as we read through the Scripture, we can draw our prayer from the passage at hand. The freshness of such prayer helps us discover the joy of a full-orbed prayer life based on Scripture itself.

Not all passages contain an example to follow, a sin to avoid, a command to obey, a promise to claim, a new thought about God, a difficulty to explore and a matter for prayer; but each includes some of these. If you'll take fifteen minutes tomorrow morning, or even today, to meet with God and look for answers to these questions in some passage of Scripture, I guarantee you a rewarding search.

The next problem is what to read for a balanced spiritual diet. Perhaps, like many other Christians, you tend to range among the Psalm 23, the Gospel of John and a few other favorite passages. Fearing the unfamiliar, you let the rest of the Bible go by default. Yet as Christians who must come to grips with the whole counsel of God, we need a planned system for reading through the whole Bible. This is the goal of *Search the Scriptures* and *This Morning with God* (InterVarsity Press). Tyndale House Publishers offers *The One Year Bible,* which is a complete Bible rearranged into daily readings from the Old Testament, New Testament, Psalms and Proverbs.[1] Whether we follow someone else's system or devise our own, it is essential that we follow some plan.

Wandering thoughts and other distractions may also plague us. That physics exam or the ball game or some coming event proves so absorbing we can't concentrate. Keeping pencil and paper handy to write down new facts and ideas met in reading is one of the best cures for this problem. Notes taken in our quiet times become a record of fresh, firsthand discoveries with God. Incidentally, these faithfully kept notes may be a lifesaver if, unexpectedly, we're called on to give a fifteen-minute devotional message. Further, our words will have the warmth and power of genuine experience as we relate a recent discovery made in personal fellowship with God.

We need to be reminded that we can't evaluate our quiet times by the way we feel afterward. Some days an idea seems to leap off the page at us and really "hits home" or leaves us with a warm glow inside. Have you ever had this happen and thought, "Ah, this morning I've met with God"? But the next few days as you read the Bible, nothing comparable happened, and you began to have that letdown feeling.

We need to realize that a right evaluation of our quiet times has nothing to do with emotional responses, which change so easily. A right evaluation is based, instead, on our recognition of the fact that God, who never changes, has met with us.

Prayer

The other vital part of our secret fellowship with God is prayer. It is just as necessary as Bible reading, if our inner lives are going to result in outward lives of spiritual power. We noted in passing that drawing from the Scriptures can freshen and vitalize a prayer life that's gone stale. Now we need to become more specific.

I'm sure we could all name the different aspects of prayer: worship, thanksgiving, confession, intercession for others and petition for ourselves. But few of us even begin to give equal time to each aspect. As I do, you probably have gimme-itis: "Gimme, gimme, gimme! Lord, I need this. I just have to have that." And you probably tend to be weakest in worshipful praying. We seldom take time quietly, alone in his presence, to realize and acknowledge the worth-ship of God. To worship is to acknowledge the character of God himself—not for what we can get out of either him or our acknowledgment of him but to acknowledge him for himself. We who aren't very good at worshiping can "prime the pump" by turning to some great hymn of the church and making its words our own expression of worship. When I'm spiritually dry, I often choose a psalm (like 103) or a hymn by one of the great saints of the past. For instance:

Join all the glorious names of wisdom, love, and power
That ever mortals knew, that angels ever bore—
All are too mean to speak his worth,
Too mean to set my Savior forth.

Or Bernard of Clairvaux's centuries-old expression:

Jesus, Thou Joy of loving hearts,
Thou Fount of life, Thou Light of men,
From the best bliss that earth imparts
We turn unfilled to Thee again.

As we share the spiritual experiences of these saints of the past, our own hearts well up in praise, adoration and worship to the living God. Such worship brings us into the presence of God, lost in wonder, caught up in what Dr. Tozer called "the gaze of the soul."

Establish Priorities

You can't worship like this in the last two minutes before dashing off to class. The major lack in our American "society of leisure" is time; we never seem to have enough. In the East, the art of meditation has been widely cultivated, but even there modern technology is robbing people of their solitude. But everyone still has twenty-four hours in each day. And most of us have a measure of control over many of those hours. Usually we can find time for what we want, even if we have to take time from another activity. The most crucial battle in our lives is the continuing one of securing enough time alone in the presence of God. Our spiritual vigor and vitality in everything else depend on the outcome of this battle.

Just as Satan uses every possible means to sow secret sin in our lives, he will do everything in his power to prevent the development of a fruitful secret life with God. Innocent, innocuous things like assignments, a phone call, somebody wanting us to go to breakfast twenty minutes early constantly conspire to cut short or cut out our daily meeting with the living God.

One summer I had the privilege of hearing John Stott, then the rector of one of the leading Anglican churches in London. He was speaking to ministers at the great Keswick Convention in the Lake District of England. His subject was priorities. The development of our inner lives, he pointed out, is the first priority for every Christian—including the minister. But he admitted a very strange paradox in his own life: "The thing I know will give me the deepest joy—namely, to be alone and unhurried in the presence of God, aware of his presence, my heart open to worship him—is often the thing I least want to do."

We are all victims of this paradox. The basic cause lies with our enemy, for he knows that we grow in spiritual power as we spend time with God. The devil will try anything, even misdirecting our desires, to attack the source of our spiritual power. There is profound truth in the little ditty, "Satan trembles when he sees the weakest Christian on his knees."

Some people claim that spending a set time with God every day is too routine or too legalistic. Personal devotions can become legalistic or mechanical, but they don't need to. When they do, healthy discipline has been converted into bondage. Bondage suggests a thing we're forced to do, something that's an odious, hateful burden for us. Self-discipline applies to what we do voluntarily to avoid pain or to secure a benefit. For spiritual growth through secret fellowship with God, we need positive discipline—now. As one who left the campus living situation some years ago, I can assure you that maintaining the secret life with God doesn't get any easier after you graduate. If you're going to set a pattern for life, now is the time to do it.

This essential disciplined regularity does not imply ironclad rigidity. The stars won't fall out of heaven the day we skip our quiet time. We don't need to fear that everything will be lost, that we'll flunk our finals, that nothing will go right, etc., etc., just because we miss one day's quiet time. God is not a tyrant who punishes us in such a way.

However, he does expect us to take our spiritual lives as seriously as we do our physical well-being. Our bodies need food, so we eat every day. Our spiritual lives need spiritual food; we should feed our souls with the Word of God every day. If we don't get the food we need, weakness soon sets in. We can't get by for long without food in either our physical or our spiritual lives.

Although we're usually more concerned with the outward appearances, God's chief concern is with our inner lives. He wants us to realize that all evidence of outward reality in our lives springs from the inner reality which only he can give us. He knows if secret sin is robbing us of spiritual power. He knows if we're reaping the full benefits of a secret life shared with him.

The beginning of spiritual reality is total commitment to Jesus Christ, evidenced by a desire to obey him. We maintain and develop spiritual vitality through daily fellowship which results in obedience and spiritual power.

Inner spiritual reality developed by a secret life with God is essential for an effective witness to a world who has yet to meet the God who alone can satisfy their every need.

QUESTIONS FOR INDIVIDUAL OR GROUP STUDY

1. According to Paul Tournier's definition of *person* and *personage* (p. 207), why should your "person" and "personage" be the same?

2. God sees your "person" even though no one else can—does this encourage or frighten you? Why?

3. The author insists that we all have secret sins which lead to outward sin and that God sees them all. In your own life, try to trace back an outward sin to a faulty inner attitude that caused it.

4. Spiritual progress and a restored relationship with Christ

call for repentance and an apology to God. Paul Little says, "He calls us to come just as we are without one plea except the blood which the Lord Jesus shed for us" (p. 211). Do you ever fall into the trap of coming to Christ "with a plea" of your own? What is the result?

5. Robert Murray McCheyne advised: "For every look you take at yourself, take ten at Jesus Christ" (p. 212). How could such a habit improve your outlook on life?

6. The author asserts: "Someone has observed that circumstances never make or break anyone; they simply reveal the person" (p. 212). Do you agree or disagree? Why?

7. The author stresses that to guard and develop our inner lives through contact with Christ, we must make Bible study and prayer a priority. However, we can get sidetracked. What are some common ways we can get caught up in the process of Bible study and prayer and lose sight of their real purpose? How can we guard against this?

8. Books and seminars on knowing God's will will attract more interest than almost any other topic. Yet Paul Little assures us, "God clearly states his will for our character and daily life" (p. 217). Why does God's will for our future seem more interesting than God's will for our attitudes and conduct? How are they intertwined?

9. The chapter suggests ways for us to have a "balanced spiritual diet" (p. 219). Is this a problem you need to overcome in your life? How will you do it?

10. "The thing I know will give me the deepest joy—namely, to be alone and unhurried in the presence of God, aware of his presence, my heart open to worship him—is often the thing

I least want to do" (pp. 222-23). Consider committing yourself to having a regular Bible study and prayer time this week
in which you study questions and format for prayer.

Bible Study Questions

- Is there an example for me to follow?
- Is there a sin for me to avoid?
- Is there a command for me to obey?
- Is there a promise for me to claim?
- What is this particular passage teaching about God or about Jesus Christ?
- Is there a difficulty here for me to explore?
- Is there something in this passage that I should pray about today?

Prayer Format

- worship
- thanksgiving
- confession
- intercession
- personal petition

SUGGESTIONS FOR A STUDY-GROUP LEADER

1. Allow group members to share how they applied last week's study. You may want to discuss why they succeeded or failed to carry out their personal applications.
2. If time permits have group members write a letter to God, as Paul Little suggests on pages 215-16.

Notes

CHAPTER 1

[1]Allan Bloom, *The Closing of the American Mind* (New York: Simon and Schuster, 1987), pp. 26, 56.

[2]*1987 World Almanac,* p. 34.

CHAPTER 6

[1]Dorothy L. Sayers, *The Mind of the Maker* (New York: Meridian Books, 1956), pp. 20-21.

[2]J. N. Hawthorne, *Questions of Science and Faith* (London: Tyndale Press, 1960), p. 55.

[3]Keith N. Schoville, *Biblical Archaeology in Focus* (Grand Rapids, Mich.: Baker Book House, 1978), p. 156.

CHAPTER 7

[1]George Gallup Jr., *Forecast 2000* (New York: William Morrow, 1984), p. 159.

[2]*New York Times,* January 2, 1983.

[3]David Riesman, Nathan Glazer, Reuel Denney, *The Lonely Crowd* (Garden City, N.Y.: Doubleday, 1955).

CHAPTER 9

[1]Mrs. Howard Taylor, *Hudson Taylor's Spiritual Secret* (Chicago:

Moody Press, 1955), p. 160. I recommend this short biography of the founder of the China Inland Mission to you for your reading and rereading.

[2]Ibid., p. 161.

[3]Ibid., p. 156.

[4]Edward J. Carnell, *The Case for Orthodox Theology* (Philadelphia: Westminster Press, 1959), p. 31.

[5]H. L. R. Deck, "I Take Thy Promise, Lord," *Hymns*, ed. Paul Beckwith (Chicago: InterVarsity Press, 1947), p. 6.

CHAPTER 10

[1]*Search the Scriptures* is a single-volume guide that takes you through the entire Bible in three years. *This Morning with God* is an inductive approach that takes almost five years. Both are available from InterVarsity Press, P.O. Box 1400, Downers Grove, IL 60515. *The One Year Bible* is published in the Living Bible paraphrase and the New International Version by Tyndale House Publishers, P.O. Box 80, Wheaton, IL 60189.

**I V P
C L A S S I C S**

In today's information age, we are deluged with content but yearn for wisdom that will transcend the moment. IVP Classics are significant, compact books that have stood the test of time, written by trusted authors who have shaped the lives of millions.

Art and the Bible, by Francis A. Schaeffer
Baptism and Fullness, by John Stott
Basic Christianity, by John Stott
The Cost of Commitment, by John White
Escape from Reason, by Francis A. Schaeffer
How to Give Away Your Faith, by Paul E. Little
The Mark of the Christian, by Francis A. Schaeffer
Your Mind Matters, by John Stott